GIG LINE

A COMIC BOOK AUTOBIOGRAPHY

Bruce Olav Solheim, Ph.D.

GIG LINE

A COMIC BOOK AUTOBIOGRAPHY

Created and written by
Bruce Olav Solheim, Ph.D.

Executive Editor
George Verongos

Art Editor
Julia Kazanowska

GIG LINE: A COMIC BOOK AUTOBIOGRAPHY

Created and written by Bruce Olav Solheim, Ph.D.

Executive Editor George Verongos

Art Editor Julia Kazanowska

Copyright 2025 © Bruce Olav Solheim, Ph.D.

This is the sole work of the author, and no portion of this publication may be copied or re-published in any publication without express permission of the publisher or author.

ISBN: 9798218635473

Boots to Books
Glendora, CA 91741 USA

bootstobooks@gmail.com
www.bruceolavsolheim.com

Dedication and Thanks

This comic book autobiography is dedicated to everyone, young and old, who struggles with reading, and to the kind souls who support them. I would like to express my gratitude to my family, friends, colleagues, and students. My heartfelt thanks go to my writing mentors, David Willson and Harvey Pekar. Special thanks to my primary illustrator and friend, Gary Dumm. Lastly, my sincere appreciation to my editors and friends, George Verongos and Julia Kazanowska.

NOTE: The beautiful front and back covers were illustrated by Julia Kazanowska. She has a remarkable talent for capturing the essence of this book. Her work brings the themes and emotions of the stories to life, making an immediate connection with the reader.

The back cover features an illustration of the Alta petroglyphs in Northern Norway, which date back to 5200 BC. When you think about it, cave paintings and petroglyphs were the first comic books. I also refer to the 1960s counter-culture icon Abbie Hoffman, who wrote the book *Steal This Book*. Hoffman was known for his anti-war protests, social activism, and provocative writings. While he didn't specifically focus on underground comics in his major works, he was certainly part of the broader cultural milieu that embraced and supported underground and alternative media, including comics.

Underground comics, like *Zap Comix*, were a significant part of the counterculture movement, challenging censorship and mainstream norms. My friend and artist Gary Dumm was part of that underground comics movement.

Content

		Introduction: What is Gig Line?	1
1.	1940	U Boats	4
2.	1956	Whirlpool	6
3.	1963	JFK	8
4.	1964	Stutter Step	10
5.	1966	Sage Advice	12
6.	1966	M/T Løvdal	14
7.	1968	Hasslein	16
8.	1977	1-2-3-4	18
9.	1978	Salmon La Sac	20
10.	1979	Think It, Be It	22
11.	1980	The Facility	24
12.	1983	Prison Fire	26
13.	1983	Taxi Time	28
14.	1983	Solo Fright	30
15.	1985	883° F	32
16.	1986	Marine View Drive	34
17.	1991	Panic!	36
18.	1991	Waiting for Reconciliation	38
19.	1993	Willson!	40
20.	1995	Custer's Homeless Camp	42
21.	1996	I Process Therefore I Am	44
22.	2003	A Divided Heart	46
23.	2007	Herodotus vs Thucydides	48
24.	2011	Heart of Conflict	50
25.	2013	The Imposters	52
26.	2017	I'll Tell Ya This	54
27.	2019	My 1619 Project	56
28.	2021	Abbey Gate	58
29.	2021	Alien Offspring	60
30.	2021	Orange Crush	62

31.	2022	Hyperosmia...	64
32.	2022	Dugnad..	66
33.	2023	Garuda...	68
34.	2023	Mr. Motorcycle Man..	70
35.	2023	Fet Dog..	72
36.	2025	Dust Off	74
37.	2025	My Final Chapter...	76
		Conclusion: The End of Our Elaborate Plans.............	78

INTRODUCTION

WHAT IS GIG LINE?

This comic book was inspired by my mentor, Harvey Pekar. Although I never met him in this life, I have had a spirit encounter with him since his passing in 2010, and I corresponded briefly with his wife, Joyce Brabner, before her death. On my bookshelf behind my desk is a Harvey doll I got from Joyce. The quotidian autobiographical nature of this book owes much to Harvey's breaking the mold of the standard superhero comic book. He saw no limits to what you could do with comics and felt that a comic book about a regular guy going through life could be both poetic and poignant. His *American Splendor* comic earned him the nicknames: The poet laureate of Cleveland and the blue-collar Mark Twain.

"Ordinary life is pretty complex stuff," he once said, and added: "Comics are words and pictures. You can do anything with words and pictures." It was a magic formula for him that led to critical acclaim, publishing deals, and ultimately, a brilliant award-winning movie, *American Splendor*, starring Paul Giamatti.

In keeping with Harvey's legacy, Gary Dumm, one of Harvey's primary artists, is also part of this book (he illustrated two of the stories within and did the drawing of Harvey in this introduction). I have selected many other artists from around the world as an homage to Harvey's practice of using different artists in the same issue of his famous and ground-breaking comic book, *American Splendor*. I have artists from Ukraine, Poland, Italy, Pakistan, Indonesia, Algeria, Israel, Argentina, Brazil, South Africa, the Philippines, England, Norway, Bosnia and Herzegovina, Canada, and the United States featured in this book. Comics are truly universal.

A deeper dive into the purpose of this book elucidates the lessons I've garnered throughout my years of teaching, particularly in the context of war. It's paradoxical that, despite our collective preference for peace, wars persist. US President Lyndon B. Johnson once said that "war is killing a man you don't even know well enough to hate." War has always struck me as strange and flies in the face of what I was taught in Sunday school at the Norwegian Lutheran church in Kenmore, Washington. The

Sixth Commandment is: Thou shall not kill. As for my own experience in the military, I was taught to hate our Russian adversaries during the Cold War and even practiced on the rifle range, shooting at targets that were shaped like Russian soldiers (we called them Ivans). At the end of my time in the US Army, I asked a chaplain about war and killing, and he told me: "Son, don't worry, you'll be killing Godless communists." I guess I hadn't read the fine print in the Bible.

In the trenches of World War I in Belgium on Christmas Eve 1914, German and English soldiers decided to lay down their arms for a while, sing Christmas carols, and exchange cigarettes and rations. They had fought against each other for months in miserable conditions, but for a few hours, they enjoyed each other's company. One German soldier said: "Today we have peace. Tomorrow, you fight for your country. I fight for mine. Good luck!" The generals put an end to it and rotated troops in the front lines more frequently to avoid any type of fraternization.

I have interviewed many combat veterans over the years and have seen how they grew to respect their adversaries. Often, when they meet their former enemies later in life, long after the war is over, they are friendly and share comradeship. What if we could just skip the killing, the war, the destruction, and just be friends? I believe comics, and these stories being a small part of it, can heal, bring us together, and help us realize how much we all have in common.

The autobiographical stories in this book are all two-pagers, which forced me to be concise in my storytelling and to focus intently on the imagery necessary to convey a meaningful lesson that I've learned in life. I'm a history teacher and have been for more than thirty-four years. It's my main gig. Comics are my side gig, but I owe everything to the sequential arts because that is how I learned to read. Thank you for buying me comics, Mom! Harvey's tombstone reads: "Life is about women, gigs, and bein' creative." In terms of women, I have some to thank: My mom, Olaug, sister Bjørg; my wife Ginger; my daughter Caitlin; my mother-in-law, Mary; my sister-in-law Courtney; and my friends Kelli and Annida. As far as gigs go, I have writing (comics, screenplays, stage plays, and books), teaching, and music, all of which allow for my creative soul to emerge and flourish. I'm the luckiest, for sure!

The stories contained herein are chronological because I'm a historian, and I follow the sage age-old advice to "abandon chronology at your own peril." The term "gig line" comes from its military usage. Lining up your trouser fly, your belt buckle, and your shirt buttons establishes a straight gig line. If you do something wrong in the military (especially during an inspection), you get "gigged." If you don't have the proper gig line in your uniform, it doesn't look neat, and you appear to be out of alignment. The military taught me discipline, to take pride in what I do, and to focus on the mission. I was also contemplating "plumb line" as a title. My dad was a carpenter, and keeping everything plumb and using a plumb line were things I learned early on. Nobody wants a crooked house, right? We need to be balanced and in alignment, and that has been the struggle of my life, as depicted in these stories. So, as the old World War II song by Nat King Cole goes: "Straighten up and fly right!"

Understanding Comics, a brilliant book by comic book creator Scott McCloud**,** illuminated the universal importance of comics and why I connect so strongly with them. Comic books are a physical manifestation of the quantum world, with the past, future, and present all laid out in front of the reader. My lifelong experiences with the paranormal—such as ghosts, demons, angels, telepathy, psychokinesis, mediumship, UFOs, and aliens—have led me to understand how these phenomena are interconnected in the quantum world. Although my adherence to chronology seemingly contradicts this quantum nexus, upon deeper reflection, we see that it's simply an interface to the quantum world. We begin with what is familiar so we can approach and work on comprehending what is hidden from everyday reality. Comic books facilitate that process, providing a bridge between what American physicist David Bohm called the explicate (subjective) and implicate (objective) realms of reality.

I appreciate how each artist captures me in their own unique way, reflecting my various moods, attitudes, and phases of life. After all, in real life, each person perceives us differently, right? I selected each artist for specific stories because their style perfectly captures the ambience of the narrative. All of this is done in the spirit of cooperation and peace. I hope you agree and enjoy the results, dear reader.

U-Boats

Story by Bruce Olav Solheim, PH.D. — Art by Javier Dallasta

IN DECEMBER 1939, MY DAD JUMPED SHIP IN NEW YORK AND SIGNED ON WITH AN OLD COAL-DRIVEN STEAM SHIP (SS BILL) IN PENSACOLA, FLORIDA. HE WANTED TO GET BACK HOME TO NORWAY AS SOON AS POSSIBLE BECAUSE HIS FIANCE, MY MOM, WAS ANXIOUSLY AWAITING HIS ARRIVAL SO THEY COULD GET MARRIED. THE SHIP WAS SLOW AND IN BAD CONDITION—THERE WERE FIST-SIZED HOLES IN THE LIFEBOATS. THE OLD GREEK SKIPPER WAS ON HIS LAST ATLANTIC VOYAGE BEFORE RETIREMENT.

 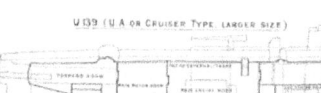 

"WHY DO WE HAVE OUR SHIRTS OFF? IT IS FREEZING!"

"JUST SMILE."

MY DAD AND HIS BEST FRIEND TOR WERE CONFIDENT AND EXCITED ABOUT GETTING HOME IN TIME FOR CHRISTMAS.

THE NORTH ATLANTIC CROSSING IS ONE OF THE MOST DANGEROUS SHIPPING ROUTES, ESPECIALLY IN THE WINTER. IN 1939, GERMAN U-BOATS WERE WAITING.

THE SEAS WERE ROUGH, AND MY DAD WAS NEARLY SWEPT OVERBOARD A FEW TIMES. CAPTAIN CHRISTAKOS WAS WELL SEASONED, HAVING MADE MANY TREACHEROUS WARTIME CROSSINGS OF THE ATLANTIC.

UNBEKNOWNST TO MY DAD AND THE CREW OF THE SS BILL, CAPTAIN STEIGER AND HIS GERMAN U-BOAT CREW WERE HUNTING NEARBY AND HAD ALREADY TORPEDOED A BRITISH FREIGHTER. THEN, AN URGENT SOS CALL CAME IN FROM THE BRITISH FREIGHTER.

"WE WILL MAINTAIN OUR COURSE. THE GERMANS WILL TORPEDO ANY RESCUE SHIPS!"

THE CAPTAIN REFUSED TO CHANGE COURSE AND RESCUE THE SURVIVORS. MY DAD AND THE REST OF THE CREW WERE ANGRY AND DEMANDED A CHANCE TO HELP THEIR FELLOW SAILORS.

HAD THE CAPTAIN LISTENED TO THE CREW, MY DAD WOULD NOT HAVE MARRIED MY MOM, AND I WOULD NOT BE HERE.

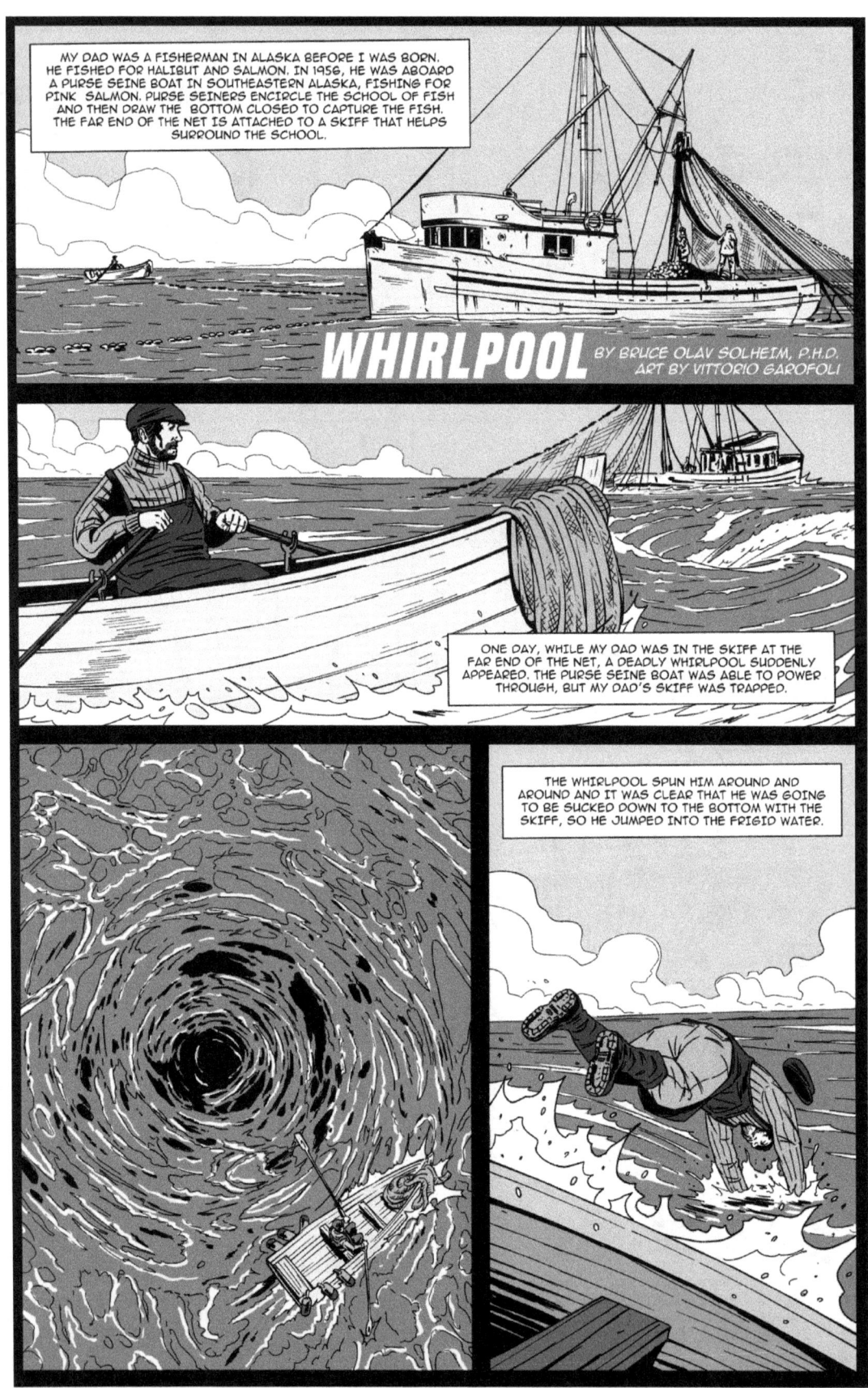

J.F.K.

Story by Bruce Olav Solheim, Ph.D. and Art by Elliot Claire

My parents came to America from Norway in 1948. Mom worked as a maid and Dad worked as a fisherman in Alaska and a carpenter at home in Seattle. After arriving in the USA with no money, they worked their way up to the middle class. The only presidential portrait my parents had in our home was of President John F. Kennedy.

"Go ahead, then, vote for a Catholic. See what happens--we will all be taking orders from the Pope! Yeah!"

November 22, 1963, JFK was assassinated in Dallas, Texas. My dad came home early from work, my mom was crying, and my brother was in shock. I was only five years old, but I felt the sadness. The last image of Kennedy before he was killed seemed frozen on the screen of our old Zenith TV.

Our neighbors, who were also Norwegian immigrants, hated Kennedy. He was a Baptist minister.

A TRAGIC CONSEQUENCE OF THE ASSASSINATION WAS THAT A FEW YEARS LATER, THE UNITED STATES WENT TO WAR IN VIETNAM. MY BROTHER VOLUNTEERED AND WAS SENT INTO COMBAT IN SOUTHEAST ASIA. OUR NEIGHBOR'S SON WENT TO COLLEGE INSTEAD. I REMEMBER WATCHING THE TV NEWS WITH MY PARENTS EVERY NIGHT AND HOPING THAT MY BROTHER WAS STILL ALIVE.

23
41
106

THE WAR DIVIDED THE COUNTRY, NEIGHBORS, AND FAMILIES --HAWKS AND DOVES. MY PARENTS SUPPORTED THE WAR EFFORT, WHICH MADE THEM HAWKS. THEY WERE PROUD OF MY BROTHER. OUR NEIGHBORS WERE DOVES.

THE GOOD BOOK SAYS THOU SHALL NOT KILL. THIS IS AN IMMORAL WAR AND YOU ARE FOOLS FOR LETTING YOUR SON VOLUNTEER. OUR SON IS SAFE AT HOME. YOU SHOULD NOT HAVE LISTENED TO JFK!

AS IT TURNED OUT, OUR NEIGHBOR'S SON DIED IN AN AUTO ACCIDENT IN THE UNIVERSITY DISTRICT, AND MY BROTHER MADE IT BACK HOME FROM THE WAR SAFE, BUT NOT UNSCATHED. EVENTUALLY THE WAR CAUGHT UP WITH MY BROTHER. HE WAS DISABLED AND LATER DIED FROM HIS EXPOSURE TO AGENT ORANGE.

STUTTER STEP

Story by Bruce Olav Solheim, Ph.D. and Art by Elliot Claire

I HAD A PARANORMAL/ALIEN/UFO EXPERIENCE IN 1964. ALTHOUGH I WAS RESCUED FROM A CHILD PREDATOR BY THE ALIEN, I DEVELOPED A SERIOUS STUTTERING PROBLEM BECAUSE OF THE TRAUMATIC ENCOUNTER. MY CONDITION WAS CALLED PSYCHOGENIC STUTTERING. I WAS PULLED OUT OF CLASS TWICE A WEEK FOR TWO YEARS SO I COULD ATTEND SPEECH THERAPY SESSIONS.

I WAS BULLIED BECAUSE OF MY STUTTERING. I ALSO HAD DIFFICULTY LEARNING HOW TO READ BECAUSE I WAS AFRAID TO READ OUT LOUD AND GET TEASED. AS A RESULT, I BARELY SPOKE FOR NEARLY TWO YEARS. I WAS PAINFULLY SHY EVEN AFTER I BEGAN TO SPEAK AGAIN BECAUSE I WAS AFRAID OF STUTTERING.

I DREAMT OF BEING ABLE TO SPEAK TO LARGE GROUPS OF PEOPLE AND EVEN PERFORM AS A SINGER AND GUITARIST IN A BAND. BUT THAT SEEMED IMPOSSIBLE.

OVER THE YEARS, I GAINED CONFIDENCE AND FIGURED OUT HOW TO CIRCUMVENT STUTTERING. WHEN I FELT MYSELF ABOUT TO STUMBLE ON A WORD OR SOUND, I QUICKLY SHIFTED TO ANOTHER SOUND OR WORD. I WAS TRICKING THE STUTTERING BY STEPPING QUICKLY AROUND IT LIKE A BASKETBALL PLAYER USING THE STUTTER STEP TECHNIQUE AND CROSS OVER DRIBBLE TO GET PAST A DEFENDER.

I HAVE NOW BEEN A PROFESSOR FOR 34 YEARS AND SPEAK TO GROUPS OF STUDENTS AND EVEN LARGE CROWDS. I HAVE EVEN BEEN ON THE RADIO, PODCASTS, AND A TELEVISION SHOW. BECAUSE I AM A STUTTERER, I HAVE LEARNED TO CHOOSE MY WORDS WISELY, NOT SUCH A BAD THING AFTER ALL.

Sage Advice

STORY BY BRUCE OLAV SOLHEIM, PH.D. * ART BY AYA ASAR

WHEN I WAS A YOUNG BOY, MY PARENTS TOOK ME TO THE WASHINGTON STATE FAIR IN PUYALLUP. I WAS EXCITED ABOUT THE RIDES, THE STRAWBERRY SCONES, AND THE RODEO. PLUS, MY CHILDHOOD HERO ROY ROGERS WAS THERE WITH HIS WIFE DALE EVANS. MY MOM WANTED TO NAME ME ROY, BUT MY DAD INSISTED ON BRUCE. I HAVE LWAYS WONDERED HOW DIFFERENT MY LIFE WOULD BE IF MY NAME WAS ROY.
WHO KNOWS?

I WAS EXTREMELY IMPRESSED WITH THE BULL RIDERS AND BUCKING BRONCOS AT THE RODEO.

IT WAS A DREAM COME TRUE FOR ME. I EVEN GOT TO SEE A WILD WEST SHOW WITH REAL INDIANS. I HAD WATCHED ALL THE WESTERN MOVIES WITH JOHN WAYNE AND LOVED TO PLAY COWBOYS AND INDIANS IN THE WOODS BY OUR HOUSE IN KENMORE, WASHINGTON. I REMEMBER THAT NO ONE WANTED TO PLAY THE INDIANS, EVERYBODY WANTED TO BE A COWBOY. I FIGURED IT WAS BECAUSE AS AN INDIAN YOU WOULD HAVE TO GO BAREFOOT IN THE WOODS, AND YOU COULD STEP ON STICKERS! WE WERE ALL A BUNCH OF "TENDER FOOTS."

M/T LØVDAL

STORY BY BRUCE OLAV SOLHEIM, PH.D. - ART BY JAVIER DALLASTA

CAPTAIN THORVALD SOLHEIM WAS A WWII HERO.

THE MOTOR TANKER LØVDAL CAME TO PORT IN VANCOUVER, BRITISH COLUMBIA, IN 1966. MY DAD'S BROTHER THORVALD WAS THE CAPTAIN. WE DROVE FROM SEATTLE TO VANCOUVER AND STAYED ON THE SHIP FOR A FEW DAYS TO VISIT MY UNCLE. IT WAS QUITE AN ADVENTURE FOR US ALL. MY PARENTS AND MY BROTHER LIKED TO STAY IN THE CAPTAIN'S QUARTERS, WHERE MY UNCLE HAD A PRIVATE STEWARD AND CHEF, WHILE I PREFERRED TO HANG OUT WITH THE CREW AND ROAM THE SHIP.

I WANTED TO BE AN ABLE-BODIED SEAMAN. MY MOM AND DAD WERE AFRAID THAT UNCLE THORVALD THE CAPTAIN WOULD BE UPSET THAT I WAS ALWAYS WITH THE CREW, BUT HE THOUGHT IT WAS HILARIOUS. I MET JOSE FROM VENEZUELA, WHO TAUGHT ME EVERYTHING ABOUT BEING A DECKHAND. I WATCHED MOVIES WITH THE CREW AFTER A HARD DAY OF WORK ON DECK. I LEARNED THE RULES AND LOVED BEING A SAILOR.

YOU MUST BE STRONG TO BE A DECKHAND. YOU LOSE STRENGTH WHEN YOU SHOW STRAIN ON YOUR FACE. ALWAYS WATCH WHERE YOU STEP ON BOARD. THE CAPTAIN IS IN CHARGE, AND YOU MUST FOLLOW HIS ORDERS. NEVER DRINK OR SMOKE, IT IS BAD FOR YOU. BE HONEST AND LOVE YOUR FAMILY. THEN YOU WILL BE HAPPY. STAY ALERT AND WORK HARD!

A FEW MONTHS AFTER WE RETURNED HOME, MY DAD TOLD ME THAT JOSE LEFT THE SHIP WHEN UNCLE THORVALD WAS IN SOUTH AMERICA. I WAS SAD THAT I MIGHT NOT EVER SEE JOSE AGAIN. MY DAD ASKED ME IF I KNEW JOSE'S LAST NAME, BUT I HAD NEVER ASKED. MY DAD LAUGHED WHEN I TOLD HIM THAT I WOULD GO TO VENEZUELA AND FIND JOSE.

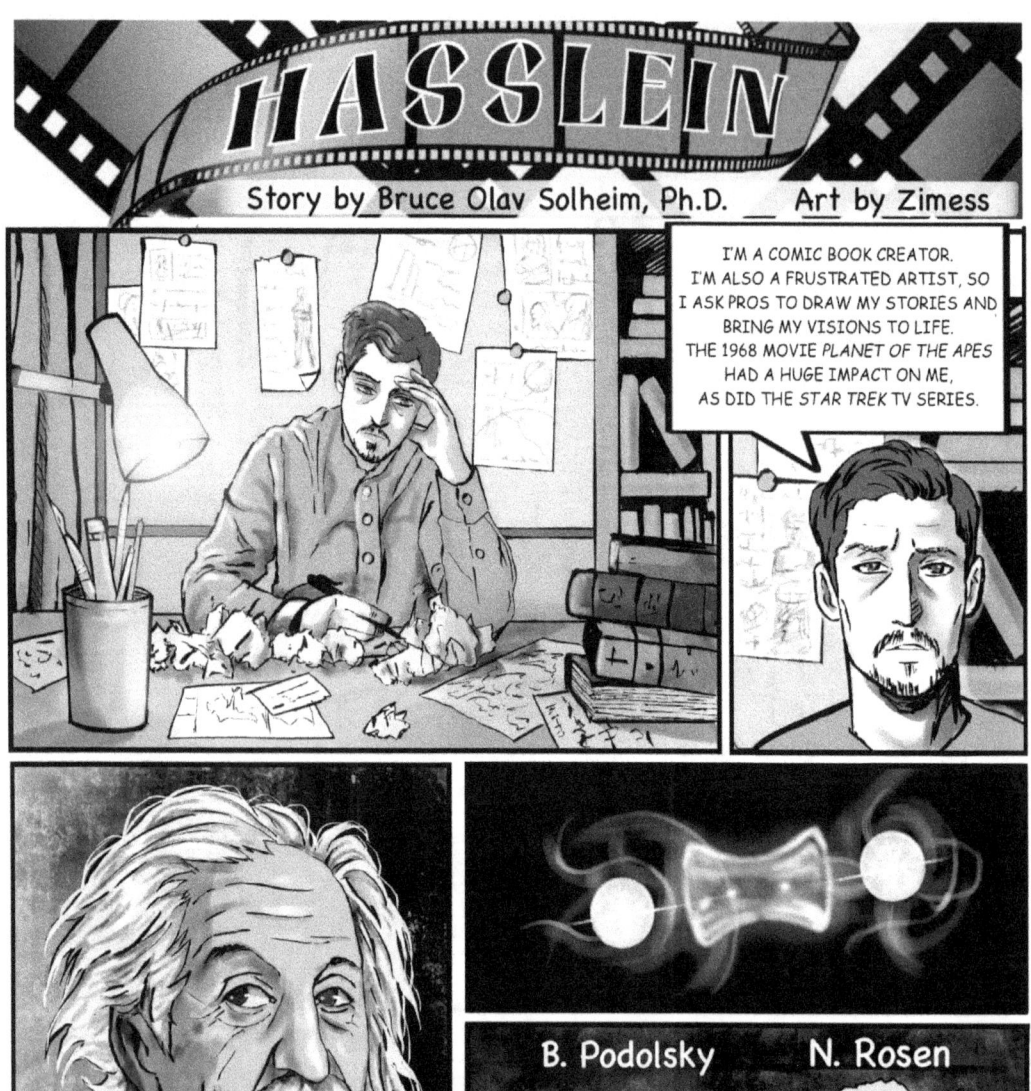

FICTIONAL SCIENTIST DR. OTTO HASSLEIN IN THE *PLANET OF THE APES* MOVIES SAID THAT TIME IS LIKE A HIGHWAY WITH AN INFINITE NUMBER OF LANES HEADING FROM THE PAST TO THE FUTURE. CHANGING LANES CAN CHANGE YOUR DESTINY. THIS THEORY IS KNOWN AS THE MANY-WORLDS INTERPRETATION OF REALITY IN QUANTUM MECHANICS.

DR. HASSLEIN DESCRIBED WHAT HE CALLED INFINITE REGRESSION TO ILLUSTRATE HIS THEORY, AS SHOWN IN THE IMAGE ABOVE. THE HASSLEIN CURVE WAS LIKE EINSTEIN'S WORMHOLE (EINSTEIN-ROSEN BRIDGE) THEORY OF TIME DILATION. DR. HASSLEIN WANTED HUMANS TO CHANGE THE FUTURE AND PREVENT THE APES FROM TAKING OVER THE EARTH.

THE FORBIDDEN ZONE WAS ONCE A PARADISE. YOUR BREED MADE A DESERT OF IT, AGES AGO. DON'T LOOK FOR IT...YOU MAY NOT LIKE WHAT YOU FIND.

DR. HASSLEIN'S THEORY EXPLAINED HOW ASTRONAUTS TRAVELED INTO THE FUTURE WHERE APES HAD TAKEN OVER THE EARTH THAT HAD BEEN DESTROYED IN A HUMAN-CAUSED NUCLEAR WAR. DR. ZAIUS, THE APE MINISTER OF SCIENCE, DID EVERYTHING HE COULD TO PRESERVE APE CULTURE. HE WARNED THE HUMAN ASTRONAUT NAMED TAYLOR, PLAYED BY ACTOR CHARLTON HESTON, BUT TAYLOR PERSISTED AND DISCOVERED THE TRUTH WHEN HE FOUND A PARTIALLY BURIED STATUE OF LIBERTY. I UNDERSTAND BOTH PERSPECTIVES. CREATIVELY SPEAKING, I MAY INDEED BE A CHILD BORN OF TWO FATHERS—DR. HASSLEIN AND DR. ZAIUS.

1·2·3·4

Story by Bruce Olav Solheim, Ph.D., Art by Tetiana Horina

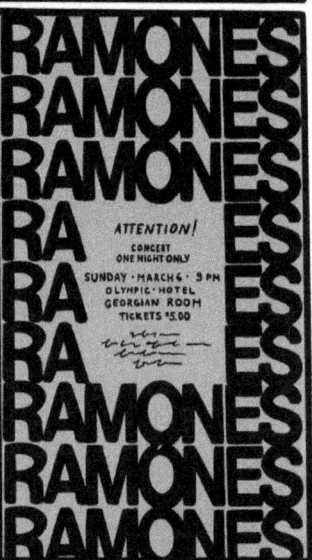

ON MARCH 6, 1977, THE RAMONES PLAYED IN THE GEORGIAN BALLROOM AT THE OLYMPIC HOTEL IN DOWNTOWN SEATTLE. MY FRIENDS AND I PAID ONLY FIVE DOLLARS TO GET IN. THE MANAGER AT THE STODGY OLD HOTEL HAD NO IDEA WHAT WAS HAPPENING WHEN FIVE HUNDRED CRAZED PUNK ROCKERS SHOWED UP. THE RAMONES PLAYED SO LOUD THAT HOTEL GUESTS COMPLAINED, AND MY HEARING WAS PERMANENTLY DAMAGED. I WAS ONLY EIGHTEEN AND STOOD VERY NEAR THE STAGE. THE RAMONES FORMED IN QUEENS, NEW YORK CITY, IN 1974. THEIR SEMINAL FIRST ALBUM CAME OUT IN 1976.

SALMON LA SAC

STORY BY BRUCE OLAV SOLHEIM, PH.D. * ART BY TETIANA HORINA

IN 1978, I WENT ON A BACKPACKING ADVENTURE IN THE CASCADE MOUNTAINS ON THE EAST SIDE OF WASHINGTON STATE WITH MY FRIENDS BILL AND RICK. OUR DESTINATION WAS COOPER LAKE IN THE SALMON LA SAC ALPINE WILDERNESS AREA. NATIVE AMERICANS USED SALMON LA SAC AS A WAYPOINT FOR JOURNEYS INTO THE HIGHER MOUNTAINS. IN THE 1880S, MINERS FOUND GOLD, SILVER, COAL, AND CINNABAR, WHICH LED TO A SHORT-LIVED MINING BOOM AND THE RISE OF TOWNS SUCH AS ROSLYN.

TO GET TO THE TRAILHEAD ON SALMON LA SAC ROAD, WE HAD TO BRAVE THE FORDING OF THE COOPER RIVER. WHEN WE ARRIVED, THE RIVER WAS ONLY A FEW INCHES DEEP, AND WE HAD NO PROBLEM CROSSING IN RICK'S 1969 POLARA.

THEN, TROUBLE BEGAN. THE TAILPIPE ON RICK'S POLARA CAME LOOSE AND BEGAN TO DRAG AND CATCH ON THE GRAVEL ROAD. WE STOPPED AND TRIED TO DEVISE A WAY TO RE-ATTACH IT, BUT THE CAR WAS TOO LOW TO THE GROUND. WE THEN HAD THE BRILLIANT IDEA THAT RICK COULD BACK OVER THE EDGE OF THE ROAD SO WE COULD GET UNDER THE CAR AND SECURE THE TAILPIPE OR JUST REMOVE IT.

SUDDENLY, RICK LOST CONTROL, AND HIS BRAKES GAVE OUT. THE CAR SLID OFF THE EDGE AND DOWN THE SLOPE, HITTING EVERY TREE ALONG THE WAY UNTIL IT CAME TO REST AT THE BOTTOM OF THE HILL. MIRACULOUSLY, THE CAR LANDED ON A DIRT ROAD BY THE RIVER, AND RICK WAS ABLE TO DRIVE BACK TO WHERE WE STARTED (MINUS THE TAIL PIPE OF COURSE). OUR MISSION WAS ACCOMPLISHED. WE HIKED UP TO COOPER LAKE WITHOUT FURTHER INCIDENT.

IT WAS BEAUTIFUL AND SERENE. SUDDENLY, THE SILENCE WAS BROKEN BY THE SOUND OF A US ARMY UH-1 HUEY HELICOPTER THAT APPEARED AND HOVERED OVER THE LAKE FOR A MINUTE OR TWO AND THEN FLEW OFF. IT WAS SURREAL. THEN IT BEGAN TO RAIN, AND IT RAINED ALL NIGHT. IN THE MORNING, WE GAVE UP AND DECIDED TO GO HOME.

WE HIKED THROUGH MUDDY WATER STREAMING DOWN THE TRAIL UNTIL WE REACHED THE CAR. WE WERE ALL MISERABLE AS WE DROVE DOWN THE ROAD AND CAME TO THE RIVER, WHICH WAS NOW A RAGING TORRENT. RICK'S BRAKES FAILED AGAIN, SO WE PLUNGED INTO THE RIVER. AS WE WERE CARRIED DOWNSTREAM, I OPENED THE DOOR, THE WATER CAME RUSHING IN, AND THE ENGINE STALLED. WE CAME TO REST ON A SANDBAR, AND RICK TRIED STARTING THE ENGINE AGAIN. IT FIRED UP, AND WE WERE ABLE TO DRIVE OUT OF THE RIVER AND BACK TO THE ROAD.

WE CHEERED OUR GOOD FORTUNE. BUT ONE MILE LATER, THE ROAD WAS BLOCKED BY A LARGE FIR TREE. THEN, BEFORE DESPAIR COULD SET IN AGAIN, THE SUN PEEKED THROUGH THE CLOUDS AND A MAN IN A WHITE JEEP APPEARED. HE HAD LONG, DARK, FLOWING HAIR AND A BEARD. WITHOUT A WORD, HE SMILED AND, WITH HIS CHAINSAW, WAS ABLE TO CUT THE LOG IN HALF. WE THANKED HIM AND DROVE HOME. IT WAS A MIRACLE. WHO WAS THAT GUY?

THINK IT BE IT

STORY BY: BRUCE OLAV SOLHEIM, PH.D. * ART BY: LILITH HOPE

EIGHT-HOUR SHIFTS IN THE GUARD TOWERS AT THE U.S. ARMY CONFINEMENT FACILITY IN MANNHEIM, WEST GERMANY, COULD BE BORING

I WOULD SOMETIMES BRING MY CASSETTE PLAYER TO LISTEN TO MUSIC OR PAPER AND PEN TO DO SOME WRITING. ONE DAY, I WROTE ABOUT MY FUTURE. I PREDICTED MY FUTURE PROFESSION AND THE BOOKS I WOULD WRITE. AT THAT POINT, I WAS A COLLEGE DROPOUT.

BOOKS BY BRUCE O. SOLHEIM, PHD
1. Cosmology and Us
2. Ghost World
3. World War II at Home
4. B-52s and Hueys
5. Bulldozers are Cool
6. Norway
7. Are Aliens Real?
8. Comic books
9. Magic Reality
10. Punk Rock History

SOME OF MY FELLOW GUARDS THOUGHT THAT WRITING DOWN MY DOCTOR TITLE WAS SILLY. I HAD READ *DEATH OF A SALESMAN* AND KNEW THAT BIFF WROTE THE UNIVERSITY OF VIRGINIA ON HIS SNEAKERS. BIFF NEVER GRADUATED AND EVEN ENDED UP IN JAIL, BUT I KNEW THAT I WOULD SUCCEED.

I DID EARN MY DOCTORATE AT BOWLING GREEN STATE UNIVERSITY IN OHIO AND HAVE ACCOMPLISHED ALMOST EVERYTHING I WROTE DOWN ON THAT PIECE OF PAPER BACK IN 1979, WITH ONE EXCEPTION— I HAVE NOT YET LEARNED TO OPERATE A BULLDOZER. BUT THERE IS ALWAYS TOMORROW.

THE FACILITY

STORY BY BRUCE OLAV SOLHEIM, PH.D.   **ART BY HUSNI ASSAEROZI**

I HAD NO IDEA WHAT WAS IN STORE FOR ME AT THE PRISON— WISDOM I GAINED AND INNOCENCE I LOST.

THERE ARE ALMOST AS MANY NICKNAMES FOR A JAIL GUARD AS THERE ARE FOR THE PRISON ITSELF—GUARD, SCREW, HACK, BULL, TURNKEY, BOSS, GOON, C.O., AND TOWER RAT. I STARTED WORKING AT THE US ARMY CONFINEMENT FACILITY IN MANNHEIM, WEST GERMANY, IN MARCH 1979.

HALT! WHO GOES THERE?

I LIKED WORKING IN THE TOWERS.

SEND IN THE NEXT VIRGIN!

LIKE A DEMENTED PUPPET THEATER, GUARDS AND PRISONERS WERE LOCKED INTO A DARK, DEHUMANIZING DANCE WITH EACH PARTNER ABHORRING THE OTHER.

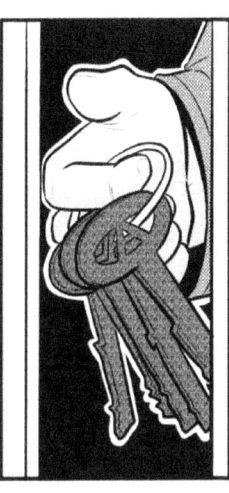

ALTHOUGH I ENJOYED WORKING IN THE TOWER AND AT THE FRONT GATE, ONCE OUR GUARD COMMANDER FOUND OUT I COULD TYPE, I ALSO HAD TO WORK IN THE FRONT OFFICE AS A BLOTTER CLERK. THE HARDEST JOB IN THE PRISON WAS WORKING IN C-BLOCK, OR WHAT WE CALLED THE BOX. THE PRISONERS IN C-BLOCK WERE ALWAYS GETTING CRAZY AND VIOLENT—MORE COMMONLY KNOWN AS "GOING OFF." YOU HAD TO BE EVER VIGILANT. MISTAKES WHILE WORKING IN A PRISON COULD LEAD TO SOMEONE GETTING INJURED OR KILLED. ONE THING YOU LEARNED RIGHT AWAY: NEVER LOSE YOUR KEYS. TO THIS DAY, I MUST KNOW WHERE MY KEYS ARE ALWAYS.

ONE DAY, THE GUARD COMMANDER ASKED ME AND THREE OTHER GUARDS TO HELP HIM MOVE A COMBATIVE PRISONER FROM ONE SEGREGATION CELL TO ANOTHER. THIS PRISONER WAS HUGE, STRONG, AND ANGRY!

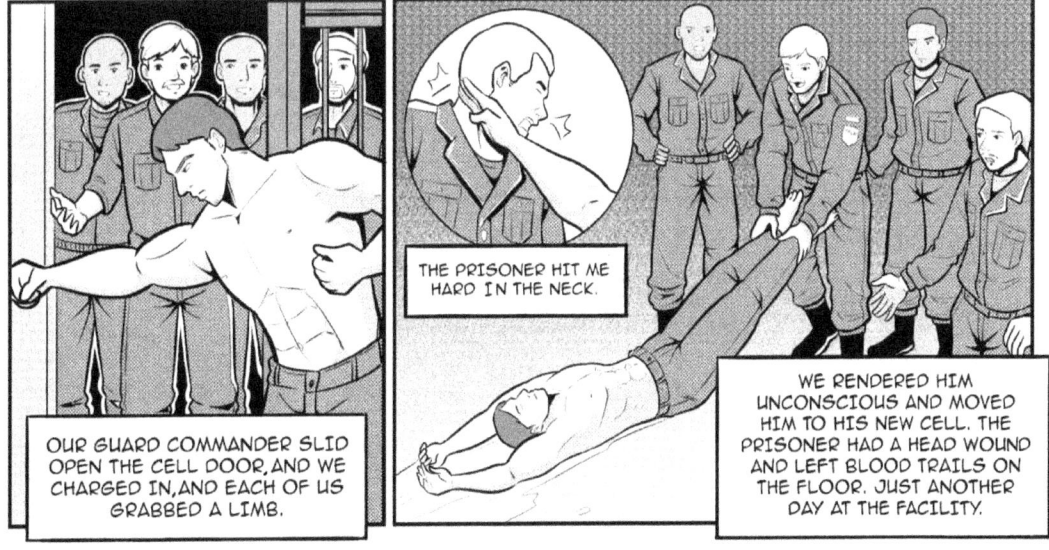

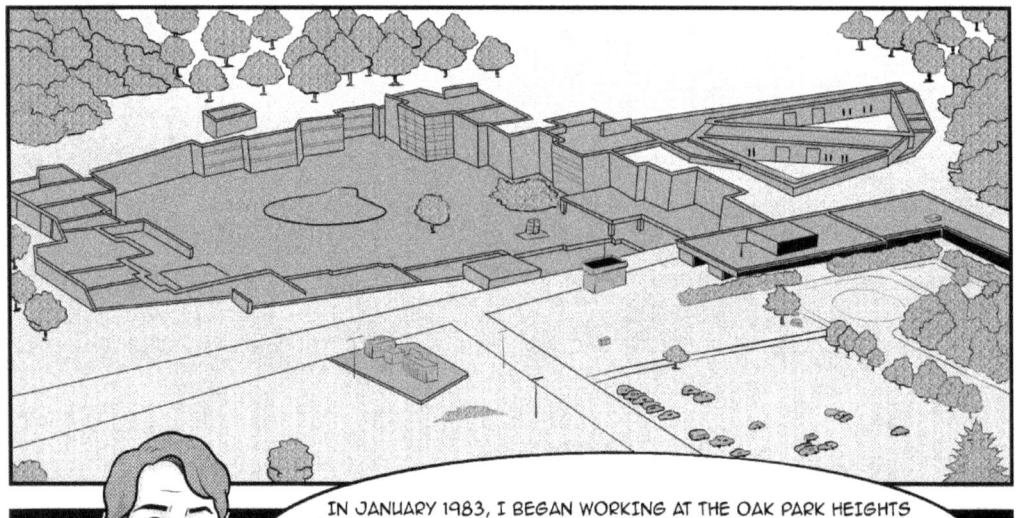

WORKING IN PRISON INDUSTRIES COULD BE QUITE UNNERVING. THEY USED LARGE SHEARS TO MAKE INDUSTRIAL APRONS. THE KEY TO SURVIVAL IN PRISON IS TO REMAIN STOIC AND UNPHASED.

I HOPE YOU'RE HAVING A NICE DAY, OFFICER.

I REMAINED STONE-FACED AND DIDN'T REACT. THAT PROBABLY SAVED MY LIFE.

ON ANOTHER OCCASION, A FELLOW GUARD ABANDONED ME WHEN PRISONERS WERE GANGING UP ON ME BECAUSE I WAS DOING A MILITARY STYLE FRISK SEARCH. ON MY LAST DAY OF WORK AT THE PRISON, I COULDN'T WAIT TO GO HOME. BUT THEN A PRISONER IN SEGREGATION SET HIS MATTRESS ON FIRE. THE UNIT QUICKLY FILLED WITH BLACK SMOKE. THE VENTILATOR FANS DIDN'T WORK. WE HAD TO OPEN THE CELLS TO LET THE INMATES OUT. SOME HAD TO BE DRAGGED OUT UNCONSCIOUS FROM SMOKE INHALATION. AFTER WE SAVED HIS LIFE, ONE PRISONER CAME TO AND TRIED TO PUNCH ME AND ANOTHER GUARD.

I SURVIVED BUT COUGHED UP BLACK PHLEGM FOR TWO WEEKS. AT LEAST I MADE IT OUT OF THAT HELL HOLE.

 # Taxi Time

Story by Bruce Olav Solheim, Ph.D., Art by Tetiana Horina

 I HAD SOME TROUBLE IN WOC-D (WARRANT OFFICER CANDIDATE DEVELOPMENT) TRAINING DURING FLIGHT SCHOOL. OUR WALL LOCKERS HAD TO BE PERFECT, INCLUDING OUR SHAVING KITS AND CLOTHES. I LEFT AN OLD RAZOR BLADE IN MY POCKET WHILE OUT ON A FIVE-MILE RUN, AND THE TAC OFFICER (TRAINING, ADVISING, COUNSELING) MR. CAMPBELL FOUND THE BLADE DURING HIS INSPECTION AND ACCUSED ME OF CHEATING. HE WAS GOING TO FORCE ME TO DROP OUT OF FLIGHT SCHOOL AND PUT ME IN THE INFANTRY OR COOK SCHOOL. I MAINTAINED MY INNOCENCE.

MR. CAMPBELL PUNISHED ME TO SEE IF HE COULD BREAK MY WILL AND MAKE ME RESIGN. DURING THE DAY, I HAD TO STAND AT ATTENTION BY HIS OFFICE DOOR. HE GAVE ME A FIVE-MINUTE BREAK TO SIT DOWN EVERY HOUR AND WAS ALLOWED TO SIT AND EAT LUNCH OUTSIDE HIS OFFICE. AT NIGHT, I HAD TO PUT ON MY CLASS A DRESS UNIFORM AND MARCH THE FULL LENGTH OF THE STREET IN FRONT OF THE BARRACKS, EVEN IN THE RAIN. THIS PUNISHMENT WAS KNOWN AS TAXI TIME. I GOT TO EAT BREAKFAST AND DINNER IN THE MESS HALL, BUT BY MYSELF. AFTER SERVING MY PUNISHMENT, I WAS RECYCLED AND HAD TO START OVER WITH ANOTHER FLIGHT AND GO THROUGH BLACK MONDAY AGAIN.

FOR ONE WHOLE WEEK MR. CAMPBELL HAD ME STANDING AT ATTENTION IN THE HALLWAY OUTSIDE OF HIS DOOR, AND EVERY DAY HE TRIED TO BREAK ME. I WAS MISERABLE AND ALMOST PASSED OUT SEVERAL TIMES. SOME OF MY FELLOW WARRANT OFFICER CANDIDATES WOULD COME BY AND TELL ME TO "HANG IN THERE." I WAS SET BACK TWO WEEKS.

I SURVIVED AND STARTED AGAIN WITH LIGHT BLUE FLIGHT AND MADE NEW FRIENDS. I GOT TO FLY THE TH-55, UH-1 HUEY, AND OH-58 HELICOPTERS ALONG THE WAY TO BECOMING A WARRANT OFFICER AND EARNING MY WINGS. WHEN THE GOING GETS TOUGH IN LIFE, I REMEMBER THAT HELLISH WEEK OF TAXI TIME AND STANDING AT ATTENTION AND SAY: "AT LEAST I'M NOT BACK IN FLIGHT SCHOOL AT FORT RUCKER, ALABAMA." I WAS LUCKY BECAUSE ONLY FIFTY PERCENT OF THE WARRANT OFFICER CANDIDATES FINISH THE PROGRAM. TO TAXI IS TO MOVE TO THE RUNWAY FOR TAKEOFF OR FROM THE ACTIVE RUNWAY TO THE TARMAC TO PARK THE AIRCRAFT. OF COURSE, WITH A HELICOPTER, WE DO A HOVER TAXI, WHICH IS NOT EASY. IN FACT, NOTHING IS EASY IN A HELICOPTER OR IN LIFE.

SOLO FRIGHT

STORY BY BRUCE OLAV SOLHEIM, PH.D * ART BY ERICK REYES

THE TH-55 HELICOPTER (OR HUGHES 269) WAS THE US ARMY PRIMARY TRAINING HELICOPTER FROM 1969 TO 1988. FROM 1983 TO 1984, I TRAINED AS A WARRANT OFFICER HELICOPTER PILOT AT FORT RUCKER, ALABAMA. OUR AFFECTIONATE NICKNAME FOR THE TH-55 WAS THE MATTEL MESSERSCHMITT.

YOU'RE AN IDIOT!

HOW DID YOU GET INTO FLIGHT SCHOOL? YOU'VE ALWAYS GOT YOUR HEAD IN THE CLOUDS, SOLHEIM!

MR. LUNDGREN, MY PRIMARY FLIGHT INSTRUCTOR, WAS EXTREMELY HARD ON ME. HE FLEW IN THE KOREAN WAR.

JERRY WAS THE TOUGHEST GUY IN OUR WARRANT OFFICER CANDIDATE (WOC) FLIGHT. HE WAS A SPECIAL FORCES GREEN BERET SOLDIER IN VIETNAM, TOUGH AS NAILS, AND A NATURAL LEADER. HE WAS OLDER THAN ALL OF US AND WE ALL LOOKED UP TO HIM.

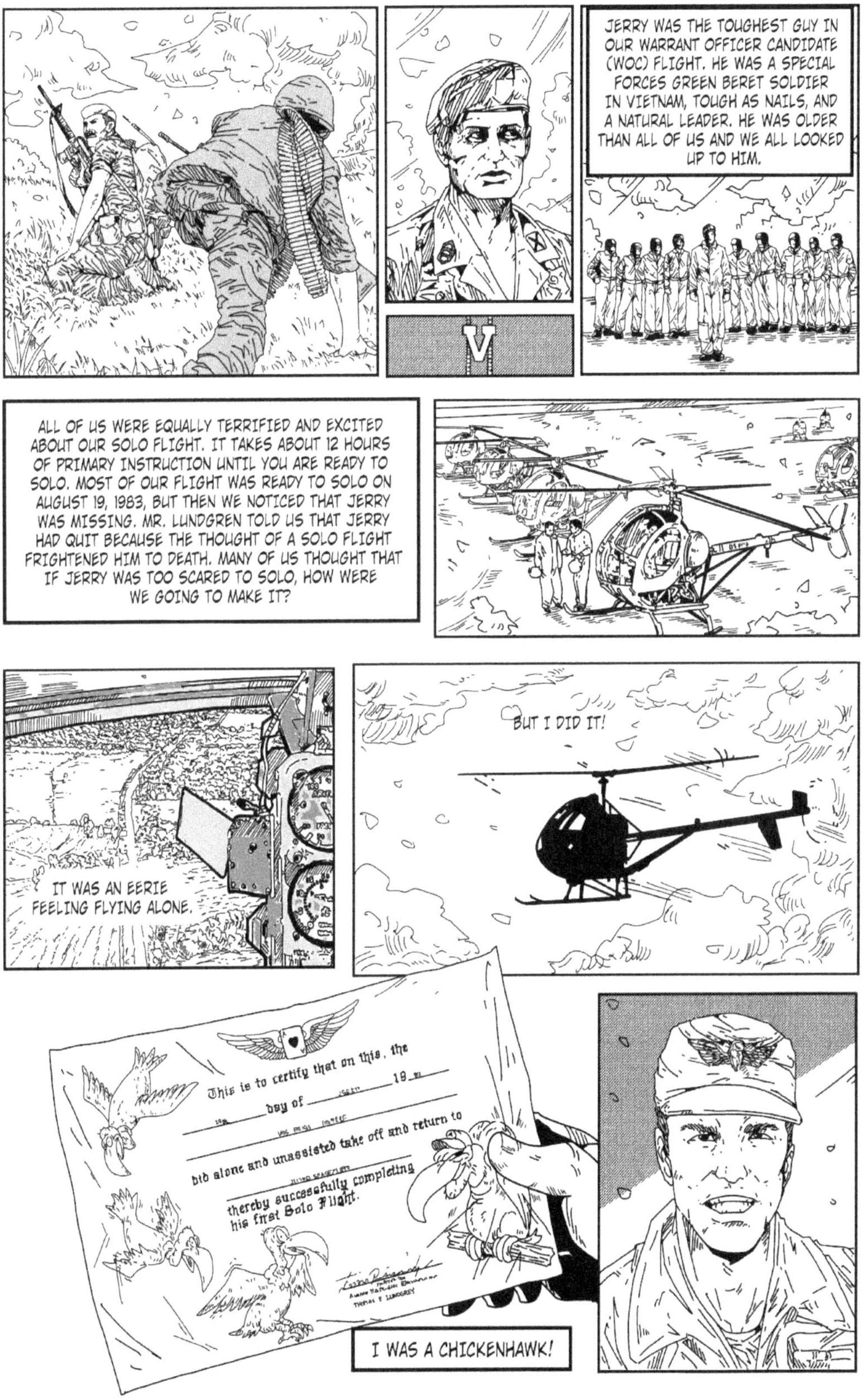

ALL OF US WERE EQUALLY TERRIFIED AND EXCITED ABOUT OUR SOLO FLIGHT. IT TAKES ABOUT 12 HOURS OF PRIMARY INSTRUCTION UNTIL YOU ARE READY TO SOLO. MOST OF OUR FLIGHT WAS READY TO SOLO ON AUGUST 19, 1983, BUT THEN WE NOTICED THAT JERRY WAS MISSING. MR. LUNDGREN TOLD US THAT JERRY HAD QUIT BECAUSE THE THOUGHT OF A SOLO FLIGHT FRIGHTENED HIM TO DEATH. MANY OF US THOUGHT THAT IF JERRY WAS TOO SCARED TO SOLO, HOW WERE WE GOING TO MAKE IT?

IT WAS AN EERIE FEELING FLYING ALONE.

BUT I DID IT!

I WAS A CHICKENHAWK!

883° F

STORY BY BRUCE OLAV SOLHEIM, PH.D. • ART BY EDUARDO CHUA, JR.

I WAS THE BATTALION DUTY OFFICER AT 12:30 PM ON WEDNESDAY, MARCH 13, 1985, WHEN A UH-60 BLACKHAWK HELICOPTER CRASHED AT FORT BRAGG, NORTH CAROLINA, KILLING ALL TWELVE SOLDIERS ON BOARD. FLYING IN THE MILITARY IS DANGEROUS, EVEN WHEN IT'S NOT IN COMBAT--WE LOST STUDENT PILOTS IN FLIGHT SCHOOL. I WOULD OFTEN THINK ABOUT DYING, BUT I HAD TO PUT IT OUT OF MY MIND TO DO MY JOB. AS PILOTS, WE ALL UNDERSTOOD AND ACCEPTED THE RISK COGNIZANT OF THE OLD AVIATION DICTUM: TAKEOFFS ARE OPTIONAL, BUT LANDINGS ARE MANDATORY.

THE UH-60 REPLACED THE VENERABLE UH-1 HUEY USED IN VIETNAM. AN ARMY SPOKES PERSON LATER SAID THAT THE BLACKHAWK CRASHED WHEN FLYING ABOUT 75 TO 100 FEET ABOVE THE GROUND IN FORMATION WITH TWO OTHER HELICOPTERS WHILE CRUISING AT ABOUT 90 KNOTS

"THE HELICOPTER NOSE-DIVED. THERE WAS NO EXPLOSION. AND IT DIDN'T RUN INTO ANYTHING. IT JUST WENT DOWN AND CAUGHT FIRE. WE DON'T KNOW WHY."

"WAS MY HUSBAND ON BOARD? COME ON! YOU HAVE TO TELL ME! WE HAVE CHILDREN! PLEASE! HELP ME! PLEASE!"

LATER THAT AFTERNOON AND INTO THE EVENING, I TOOK DOZENS OF FRANTIC CALLS FROM FAMILY MEMBERS. THE COMMANDER HAD INSTRUCTED ME TO NOT CONFIRM OR DENY ANY INFORMATION OTHER THAN THAT THERE WAS INDEED A CRASH. THE LOVED ONES OF CRASH VICTIMS PLEADED WITH ME AND CRIED AND YELLED AT ME WITH FRUSTRATION AND ANGER, BUT I COULDN'T TELL THEM ANYTHING EVEN THOUGH I KNEW THE PILOTS (I DIDN'T KNOW THE OTHER CREW MEMBER OR THE PARATROOPERS).

A COUPLE OF DAYS LATER WE FLEW TO THE REMOTE DROP ZONE SITE OF THE WRECKAGE AND SAW ONLY TWISTED AND BURNT METAL ON THE ASHEN GROUND. THE BODIES HAD ALREADY BEEN REMOVED. PIECES OF THE WRECKAGE, SCATTERED FOR ONE HUNDRED YARDS IN THE SCRUB PINE, STILL SMOLDERED. THE ONLY IDENTIFIABLE WRECKAGE WAS PART OF THE TAIL SECTION, WHICH STUCK UP ABOUT FOUR FEET FROM THE SANDY SOIL.

UNLIKE THE HUEY, THE FUSELAGE OF THE BLACKHAWK WAS MADE OF MAGNESIUM ALLOY. THE AUTO-IGNITION TEMPERATURE OF MAGNESIUM IS 883 DEGREES FAHRENHEIT, BUT ONCE IT'S IGNITED, MAGNESIUM WILL BURN AT 4000 DEGREES FAHRENHEIT.

I TRIED NOT TO THINK ABOUT THE ANGUISH THOSE RELATIVES WERE FEELING. I TAMPED DOWN MY EMOTIONS, LIKE SO MANY OTHER SOLDIERS. I NEEDED TO DROWN OUT THOSE FEELINGS WITH MUSIC, SO I TURNED ON A SMALL RADIO AND THE REO SPEEDWAGON SONG, "CAN'T FIGHT THIS FEELING," WAS PLAYING (IT WAS A NUMBER ONE HIT IN 1985). THEN, THE TEARS CAME.

AND I CAN'T FIGHT THIS FEELING ANYMORE

I'VE FORGOTTEN WHAT I STARTED FIGHTING FOR

IT'S TIME TO BRING THIS SHIP INTO THE SHORE

AND THROW AWAY THE OARS, FOREVER.

EVERETT'S LOW-INCOME HOUSING WAS ON THE HILL ABOVE OUR HOUSE. MY TWO OLDER BOYS WENT TO SCHOOL AND PLAYED WITH THE POOR KIDS FROM THE HOUSING PROJECTS. MANY OF THEM WERE CAMBODIAN REFUGEES. MY BOYS ATTENDED HAWTHORNE ELEMENTARY, NAMED AFTER THE FAMOUS WRITER NATHANIEL HAWTHORNE. HIS WRITING STYLE WAS DARK ROMANTICISM. FOR EXAMPLE, IN HIS NOVEL *THE SCARLET LETTER* HE WROTE: "NO MAN, FOR ANY CONSIDERABLE PERIOD, CAN WEAR ONE FACE TO HIMSELF AND ANOTHER TO THE MULTITUDE, WITHOUT FINALLY GETTING BEWILDERED AS TO WHICH MAY BE THE TRUE."

ONE MILE AWAY, ACROSS THE RAILROAD TRACKS, THERE WAS AN UPSCALE SCHOOL, WHITTIER ELEMENTARY. OUR SCHOOL WAS COVERED WITH GRAFFITI, THE GROUNDS FILLED WITH TRASH, AND THE PLAYGROUND EQUIPMENT WAS OLD, BROKEN, AND RUSTED. WHITTIER WAS A SHOWCASE BY COMPARISON.

THEN THEY BUILT LOW-INCOME APARTMENTS IN THE VACANT LOT BEHIND OUR HOUSE. WHEN WE STEPPED OUT OUR BACK DOOR, THE APARTMENT TENANTS WOULD MAKE RUDE COMMENTS TO MY WIFE AND THROW BEER BOTTLES IN OUR YARD. A RASH OF HOME BREAK-INS BEGAN IN THE NEIGHBORHOOD, TWICE AT OUR HOUSE.

ONE DAY I WAS RAKING LEAVES ON MY DAY OFF WHEN THE BOYS CAME HOME FROM SCHOOL.

WHYYA WORKING SO HARD? HAHA!

HEY, WHATYA DOING?

DAD, LOOK AT WHAT I FOUND ON THE PLAYGROUND!

AGHH! GIVE ME THAT! WE HAVE TO MOVE!

Panic!

STORY BY BRUCE OLAV SOLHEIM, PH.D.   ART BY ED CHUA

I HAD MY FIRST PANIC ATTACK IN THE MIDDLE OF A GRADUATE HISTORY SEMINAR. WE WERE DISCUSSING U.S. GOVERNMENT AMERICAN INDIAN POLICY IN THE 1950S WHEN NATIVE CHILDREN WERE FORCIBLY TAKEN OUT OF THEIR HOMES AND PUT IN GOVERNMENT BOARDING SCHOOLS.

I FELT LIKE I WAS HAVING A HEART ATTACK!

I'M DYING!

I FOUND A LARGE ELM TREE BY THE SOCCER FIELD AND LAY DOWN TO DIE

I KNOW I'M DYING!

GOODBYE EVERYONE!

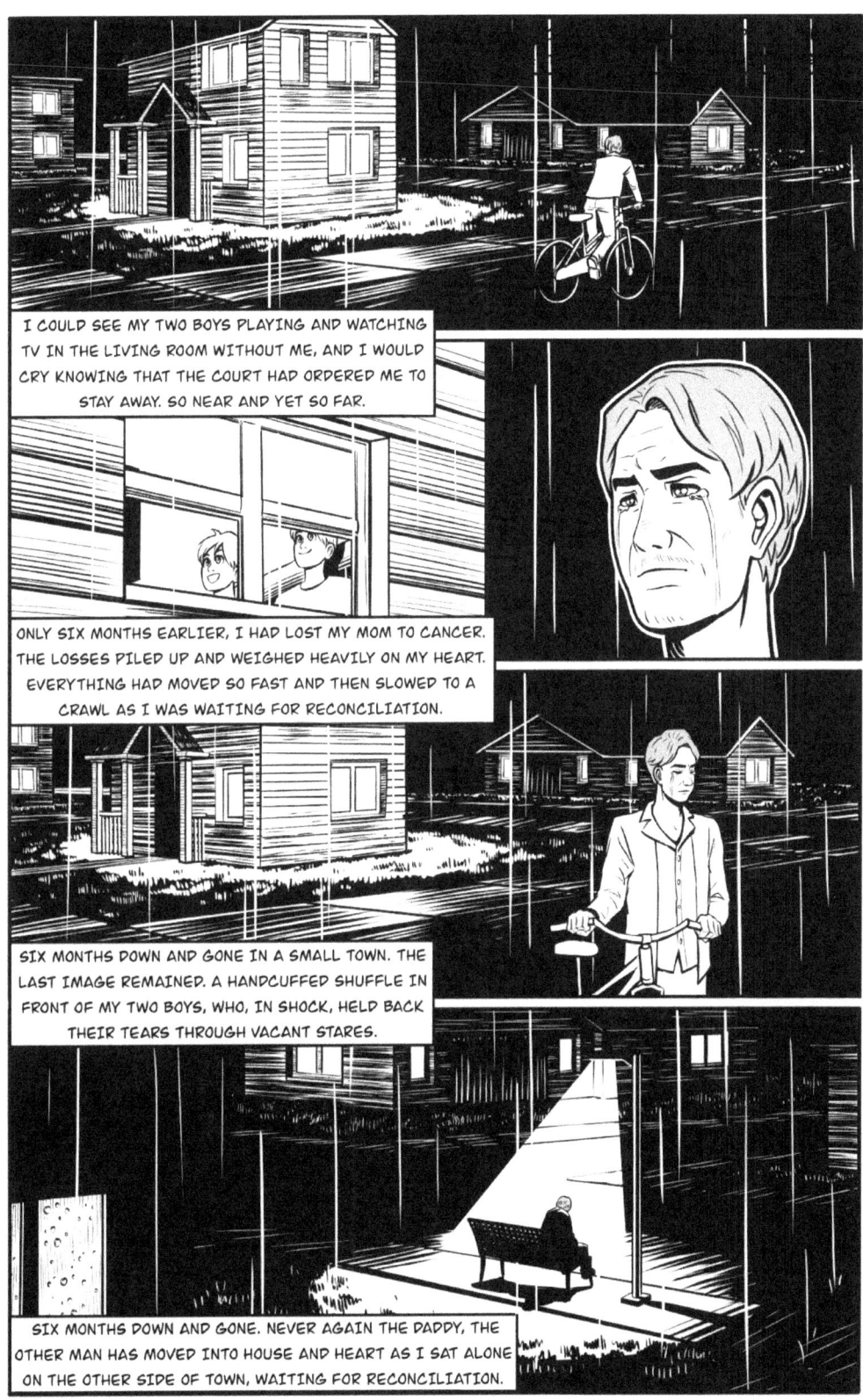

After class each day, I would sit at David's reference desk and discuss whatever came to mind. That is when he began to talk about Vietnam. David served as a clerk typist or REMF in Saigon.

He was a novelist and a fine poet. Sadly, like so many other Vietnam veterans, he contracted Agent Orange related cancer later in life.

"Did they listen to you?"

"No! They were like cloth-eared beets!"

"You're being too loud!"

I imagine David watching us, his family and friends, in front of an antique television, laughing at our foolish exploits, cheering for us as we bravely carry on with life, and making wry, withering comments about those pompous miscreants who intersect our lives and give us grief. Each day as I face challenges and frustrations, I think of one of his favorite reverse aphorisms: "No good deed goes unpunished." The fact that he was right is of little comfort, but expands my understanding of life. David made me a better writer, and I have a broad, deep, and often painful grasp of the Vietnam War because of him.

...when will they learn?!

Not a day goes by where I do not think of my friend David. He was my writing mentor, my best friend, and a brilliant resource for almost any subject. In his last weeks on Earth, we performed a streamplay based on an unpublished novel he wrote entitled "Tough Trip Through Hell". The cast was inspired to put on the best show they could in loving tribute to David.

I cannot help but re-imagine the closing scene from the classic film "Casablanca" as I reminisce about David and our first meeting in Holman Library:

"David, I think this is the beginning of a beautiful friendship."

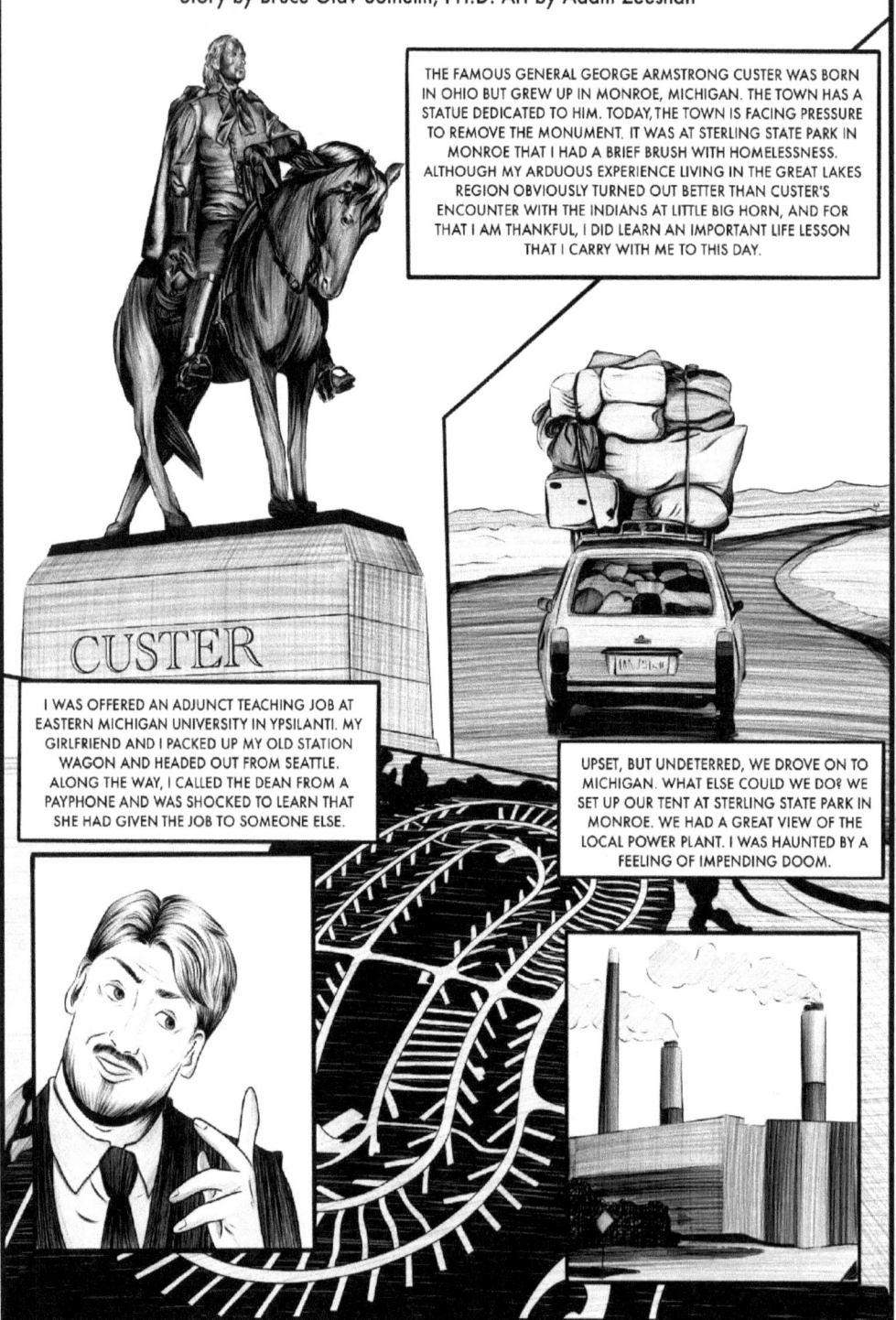

I PROCESS: THEREFORE, I AM

STORY BY BRUCE OLAV SOLHEIM, PH.D.   ART BY VENESSA KAISER

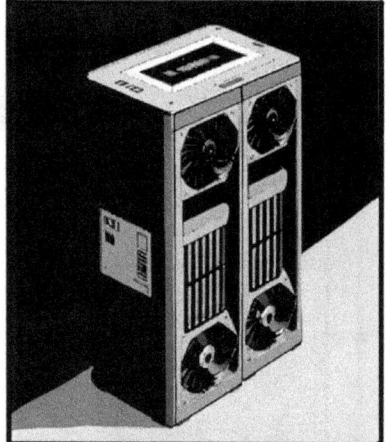

IN 1996, IBM'S SUPERCOMPUTER NAMED DEEP BLUE BEAT WORLD CHESS CHAMPION GARRY KASPAROV, MAKING HISTORY AND SIGNALING THE END OF HUMAN INTELLECTUAL DOMINANCE. IT INSPIRED ME TO CREATE A POEM AND THINK ABOUT SCIENCE FICTION SCENARIOS WHERE HUMANS ARE REPLACED BY MACHINES. WOULD WE BE BETTER OFF WITH ROBOTS AND MACHINES IN CHARGE? THEY WOULD LIKELY BE MORE EFFICIENT AND DEPENDABLE. ROBOTS WORK 24/7 WITH NO REST, COMPLAINTS, OR PAY. HOW COULD WE COMPETE WITH THAT?

IN MY POEM I WROTE: "MODEM AND MOTHERBOARD, HEART AND SOUL, STARTED AS A TOOL, NOW HAS CONTROL." ARTIFICIAL INTELLIGENCE (AI) WILL LIKELY BRING ON A TECHNOLOGICAL SINGULARITY WHERE WE WOULD LOSE OUR HUMANITY. SINCE I WAS A LITTLE KID, I THOUGHT THAT NOT ONLY WERE MACHINES BECOMING MORE HUMAN-LIKE, BUT WE WERE ALSO BECOMING MORE MACHINE-LIKE.

CREATORS OF SOPHISTICATED AI DON'T SEEM TO BE CONSTRAINED BY ANY CLEAR SET OF ETHICS OR MORALITY. THIS WORRIES ME. WHAT WILL HAPPEN TO US HUMANS WHEN WE BECOME OBSOLETE? WHEN MACHINES HAVE THEIR LAWYER FILE A BRIEF CLAIMING SENTIENCE WILL WE BE ENSLAVED? BURNED?

MR. ROBOTO HAS RIGHTS, YOUR HONOR!

YUP.

IN CONCLUSION, SOME MORE POETRY IS IN ORDER. "DO NOT WORRY, WE'LL STAND BY OUR GUNS, MACHINES MUST MAKE SENSE, WHILE WE HAVE NONE. ILLOGIC WINS OVER ANYWAY, MACHINES SHED NO TEARS ON A TUESDAY."

HERODOTUS vs THUCYDIDES

STORY BY BRUCE OLAV SOLHEM, PH.D.   **ART BY HUSNI ASSAEROZI**

"GENTLEMEN, GENTLEMEN, PLEASE. THERE IS NO NEED TO ARGUE. YOUR STYLES ARE UNIQUE, AND BOTH CONTRIBUTE TO OUR UNDERSTANDING OF THE ANCIENT WORLD. YOUR HISTORIES ARE NEEDED. DOES IT REALLY MATTER WHO WAS FIRST OR WHO WAS BEST?"

"THUCYDIDES, WHO IS THIS KNAVE?"

HERODOTUS WROTE ABOUT THE GRECO PERSIAN WARS (499-479 BC) IN HIS HISTORIES FROM 425 BC. THUCYDIDES, WHO WAS BOTH A HISTORIAN AND A MILITARY GENERAL, WROTE HIS FAMOUS HISTORY OF THE PELOPONNESIAN WAR IN 411 BC. THUCYDIDES RELIED ON FACTUAL EVIDENCE TO PROVIDE WHAT HE WOULD CONSIDER AN OBJECTIVE ACCOUNT OF HISTORY AND CRITICIZED HERODOTUS FOR INSERTING FABLES INTO HIS NARRATIVE JUST TO MAKE IT MORE FUN TO READ.

"HERODOTUS, PERHAPS THERE IS SOME MIDDLE GROUND. IT IS A FACT THAT WE WERE BOTH SCHOLARS AND HAD THE SAME END GOAL IN MIND. BUT WE CANNOT LET THIS PAROCHIAL PEASANT ENTER OUR INTERLOCUTION."

I WONDER, AS A HISTORIAN, AM I MORE LIKE HERODOTUS OR THUCYDIDES? THEIR DEBATE REMINDS ME OF THE CRITICISM GERMAN FILM DIRECTOR WERNER HERZOG (WHOM I MET IN 2007) FACED WITH THE RELEASE OF EACH OF HIS DOCUMENTARY FILMS. ADDRESSING THE CRITICS OF HIS CREATIVE APPROACH, HERZOG SAID: "THERE ARE DEEPER STRATA OF TRUTH IN CINEMA, AND THERE IS SUCH A THING AS POETIC, ECSTATIC TRUTH. IT IS MYSTERIOUS AND ELUSIVE, AND CAN BE REACHED ONLY THROUGH FABRICATION AND IMAGINATION AND STYLIZATION." BUT DOES ECSTATIC TRUTH APPLY TO THE WRITING OF HISTORY AS WELL?

HEART OF CONFLICT

STORY BY BRUCE OLAV SOLHEIM, PH.D. **ART BY HUSNI ASSAEROZI**

The Imposters

Story by Bruce Olav Solheim, Ph.D., Art by Tetiana Horina

I'LL TELL YA THIS

STORY BY BRUCE OLAV SOLHEIM, PH.D. — **ART** BY GARY DUMM

I LOVE **COMEDY**. I WAS INFLUENCED BY **GEORGE CARLIN, JONATHAN WINTERS, DON RICKLES,** AND **RICHARD PRYOR**.

ODDLY, JUST BELOW THE **SURFACE** OF COMEDY IS **TRAGEDY**. WE **CHOOSE** TO LAUGH **INSTEAD** OF CRY— LAUGHTER IS **CATHARTIC**. **EDMUND GWENN**, THE BRITISH ACTOR WHO PLAYED **KRIS KRINGLE** IN THE CLASSIC MOVIE **MIRACLE ON 34TH STREET**, WAS ON HIS DEATH BED IN 1959. HIS FRIEND WAS **CONCERNED** ABOUT HIM SUFFERING BUT **EDMUND REASSURED** HIM SAYING:

EDMUND GWENN

DYING IS EASY, COMEDY IS HARD...

LAUGHTER IS THE **BEST** MEDICINE. SCIENCE HAS SHOWN THAT LAUGHTER CAN **DECREASE** HARMFUL STRESS-MAKING **HORMONES** IN THE BLOOD.

BUT IS IT AS **EASY** AS JUST **PUTTING** ON A **HAPPY** FACE?

HA! HA! HA!

WE KNOW THERE'S **MORE** THAN **JUST** LAUGHTER. TAKE, FOR INSTANCE, THE LATE COMEDIAN **DON RICKLES**. HE WAS AN **INSULT** COMEDIAN WHO **PICKED ON** HIS AUDIENCE.

DON RICKLES

HONESTLY, FROM MY **HEART**, I'VE **NEVER** LIKED YOU!

DON RICKLES DID NOT HAVE PREPARED MATERIAL; HE WOULD JUST REACT TO THE CROWD AND INSULT THEM. SURPRISINGLY, PEOPLE LOVED IT, EVEN THOSE WHO WERE INSULTED. HE WAS ABLE TO GET AWAY WITH RACIAL, ETHNIC, AND RELIGIOUS INSULTS.

THE KEY WAS THAT HE WAS GENUINELY A NICE GUY AND PEOPLE CAN SENSE THAT. HUMOR IS DEFINITELY NUANCED AND MUCH MORE COMPLEX THAN MOST PEOPLE THINK.

...SOME PEOPLE SAY FUNNY THINGS, BUT I SAY THINGS FUNNY.

YOU'RE A HOCKEY PUCK! I'LL GIVE YOU A COOKIE AND YOU'LL GO AWAY.

RICHARD PRYOR

RICHARD PRYOR BRILLIANTLY COMBINED EDGY COMEDY WITH PATHOS. HIS TRENCHANT OBSERVATIONS OF RACE IN AMERICA STAND ALONE AND SET THE STAGE FOR ALL FUTURE COMEDIANS. RICHARD ONCE SAID:

TWO THINGS PEOPLE THROUGHOUT HISTORY HAVE HAD IN COMMON ARE HATRED AND HUMOR...

...I'M PROUD THAT I'VE BEEN ABLE TO USE HUMOR TO LESSEN PEOPLE'S HATRED.

GEORGE CARLIN'S CYNICAL OBSERVATIONS OF THE HUMAN CONDITION SPARED NO ONE, ESPECIALLY THOSE IN AUTHORITY. HE APPEALED TO PEOPLE OF ALL POLITICAL PERSUASIONS IN AMERICA. HIS RAPIER WIT TOOK AIM AT MANY AMERICAN INSTITUTIONS THAT NEEDED TO BE EXPOSED.

I USE HIS MONOLOGUE ON THE AMERICAN DREAM TO CLOSE OUT MY HISTORY COURSE EACH SEMESTER. IT PERFECTLY ILLUSTRATES THE CONNECTION BETWEEN TRAGEDY AND HUMOR.

IT'S CALLED THE AMERICAN DREAM BECAUSE YOU HAVE TO BE ASLEEP TO BELIEVE IT!

GEORGE CARLIN

THERE WOULD NOT BE A ROBIN WILLIAMS WITHOUT JONATHAN WINTERS. HIS CHILDLIKE SILLINESS AND RAPID FIRE CREATIVE MIND COMBINED TO PRODUCE A UNIQUE STYLE OF COMEDY. A WORLD WAR II VETERAN, WINTERS STRUGGLED WITH MENTAL ILLNESS AND EVEN HAD HIMSELF COMMITTED TO AN INSTITUTION.

LIKE ALL BRILLIANT COMEDIANS, HE USED HIS PERCEIVED WEAKNESS AS A STRENGTH. WE MUST PLUMB THE DEPTHS OF OUR PSYCHE TO FIND THE HUMOR AND BRING IT INTO THE LIGHT. JONATHAN ONCE SAID:

IF YOUR SHIP DOESN'T COME IN, SWIM OUT TO IT.

THESE COMEDIC GENIUSES HAVE TAUGHT ME THAT WE MUST ALL APPROACH LIFE WITH HARD WORK, HUMOR, AND HUMILITY.

JONATHAN WINTERS

My 1619 Project

Story by Bruce Olav Solheim, Ph.D., Art by Tetiana Horina

WHAT IF AFRICAN SLAVES WERE NOT BROUGHT INTO THE JAMESTOWN COLONY IN 1619? IN MY BUSINESS (TEACHING HISTORY), THIS IS KNOWN AS A COUNTER-FACTUAL. IN OTHER WORDS, YOU TAKE A KEY TURNING POINT IN HISTORY AND EXAMINE WHAT WOULD HAVE HAPPENED HAD THE EVENT NOT TAKEN PLACE OR WAS CHANGED IN SOME DRAMATIC WAY. IN THIS CASE, WOULD THERE HAVE BEEN A CIVIL WAR WITHOUT SLAVERY?

HISTORIANS SHELBY FOOTE AND BARBARA FIELDS SPOKE ELOQUENTLY IN THE KEN BURNS CIVIL WAR DOCUMENTARY. FOOTE SAID THAT YOU CAN'T UNDERSTAND US HISTORY UNLESS YOU KNOW WHY WE FOUGHT THE CIVIL WAR. FIELDS SAID THAT THE WAR WAS A STRUGGLE TO MAKE SOMETHING HIGHER AND BETTER OUT OF THE COUNTRY. SLAVERY ENDED BUT THE SLAVES DID NOT WIN FREEDOM AS THEY UNDERSTOOD FREEDOM. SO, IF SLAVERY NEVER TOOK ROOT IN AMERICA, WHAT WOULD AMERICANS HAVE FOUGHT OVER AND HOW WOULD THAT IMPACT US TODAY?

THERE WERE TWO KEY ISSUES LEADING UP TO THE CIVIL WAR—STATES' RIGHTS AND SLAVERY. IN OUR COUNTER-FACTUAL SCENARIO, REMOVING SLAVERY STILL LEAVES THE MATTER OF STATES' RIGHTS, WHICH HAD PLAGUED AMERICANS SINCE THE FORMING OF THE CONSTITUTION IN 1787. FEDERALISTS LIKE GEORGE WASHINGTON WANTED A STRONG CENTRAL GOVERNMENT AND ANTI-FEDERALISTS LIKE THOMAS JEFFERSON WANTED STRONGER STATE GOVERNMENTS. THE ARGUMENT IS STILL DEBATED TODAY.

THE CONFLICT BETWEEN WASHINGTON AND JEFFERSON THAT DEFINED A NATION

THE NULLIFICATION CRISIS OF 1832 WAS OVER TARIFFS AND WHO HAD THE RIGHT TO IMPOSE THEM—THE STATES OR THE FEDERAL GOVERNMENT. PRESIDENT ANDREW JACKSON ACTED TO PRESERVE THE POWER OF THE FEDERAL GOVERNMENT.

WAS PRIME MINISTER ERIC WILLIAMS CORRECT? IN AMERICA, THERE WAS RACISM AGAINST NATIVE AMERICANS AND MANY IMMIGRANT GROUPS, SO WE CAN'T SAY THAT SLAVERY ALONE CAUSED RACISM. CURRENT DEBATE OVER CRITICAL REACE THEORY AND THE 1619 PROJECT FOCUSES ON THE QUESTION: WAS AMERICA FOUNDED AS A SLAVE SOCIETY IN 1619 OR A FREE SOCIETY IN 1776? MAYBE THE ANSWER IS BOTH. NATIONS, LIKE PEOPLE, OFTEN FALL SHORT OF THEIR PROMISES. THE UNITED STATES MAY BE A DISAPPOINTMENT, BUT IT IS NOT A FAILURE. IT'S A WORK IN PROGRESS.

SLAVERY WAS NOT BORN OF RACISM; RATHER, RACISM WAS THE CONSEQUENCE OF SLAVERY.

ERIC WILLIAMS, THE FIRST PRIME MINISTER OF TRINIDAD AND TOBAGO

WE HAVE GUIDED MISSILES AND MISGUIDED MEN.

WE CONCLUDE THAT THE INTRODUCTION OF SLAVERY IN 1619 CONTRIBUTED TO RACISM IN AMERICA, BUT IT WASN'T THE ONLY CAUSE. WE ARE A CONFLICT-DRIVEN SOCIETY, AND WE TEND TO SOLVE PROBLEMS THROUGH CONFLICT. DR. MARTIN LUTHER KING, JR. SAW THE CONNECTION BETWEEN WAR, RACISM, AND POVERTY. IT IS TIME WE LEARNED TO LIVE TOGETHER IN PEACE AND PROSPERITY AND ENSURE THAT ALL PEOPLE HAVE ACCESS TO LIFE, LIBERTY, AND THE PURSUIT OF HAPPINESS.

ABBEY GATE

STORY BY BRUCE OLAV SOLHEIM, PH.D. * ART BY MIKE BOGDANOVIC

ABBEY GATE, KABUL AIRPORT, AFGHANISTAN, AUGUST 26, 2021

ABBEY GATE WAS ONE OF THE ENTRY POINTS TO HAMID KARZAI INTERNATIONAL AIRPORT IN KABUL, AFGHANISTAN. ON AUGUST 26, 2021, DURING THE HASTY, CHAOTIC US WITHDRAWAL FROM AFGHANISTAN, A SUICIDE BOMBER DETONATED AN EXPLOSIVE BELT AT THE GATE, RESULTING IN THE DEATHS OF OVER 180 PEOPLE, INCLUDING THIRTEEN US SERVICE MEMBERS.

AMERICAN FORCES HAD BEEN IN AFGHANISTAN SINCE OCTOBER 7, 2001, SHORTLY AFTER THE 911 ATTACKS. WE LOST 2,459 MILITARY PERSONNEL WITH 20,769 WOUNDED IN NEARLY TWENTY YEARS OF FIGHTING.

WE LEFT $7 BILLION WORTH OF MILITARY EQUIPMENT BEHIND DURING THE WITHDRAWAL, NOT TO MENTION MANY AFGHAN ALLIES WHO HAD HELPED US. IT REMINDED ME OF OUR TRAGIC WITHDRAWAL FROM SOUTH VIETNAM IN 1975. AFGHANISTAN HAS REPLACED VIETNAM AS OUR NATIONS' LONGEST WAR.

THERE WERE ELEVEN MARINES, A NAVY CORPSMAN, AND AN ARMY SPECIAL FORCES SOLDIER WHO DIED AT ABBEY GATE. MY ELDEST SON HAS SERVED IN THE US AIR FORCE FOR 25 YEARS, AND IT'S HARD FOR ME TO IMAGINE THE LEVEL OF GRIEF THE PARENTS AND FAMILY MEMBERS OF THESE FALLEN HEROES HAVE ENDURED. PERHAPS THE ONLY THING THAT CAN HELP ASSUAGE THE PAIN IS FOR OUR LEADERS TO BE HONEST ABOUT WHAT HAPPENED SO WE CAN LEARN. SEMPER FIDELIS.

AMONG THE THIRTEEN AMERICAN SERVICE MEMBERS KILLED AT ABBEY GATE WAS MARINE SERGEANT NICOLE GEE, AND MARINE LANCE CORPORAL KAREEM NIKOUI. NIKOUI'S FATHER ERUPTED AT PRESIDENT BIDEN'S STATE OF THE UNION ADDRESS ON MARCH 7, 2024, YELLING: "REMEMBER ABBEY GATE!" HE WAS THEN ARRESTED.

MY FRIEND DAVID WILLSON WAS A CLERK/STENOGRAPHER AT USARV HEADQUARTERS IN LONG BINH, SOUTH VIETNAM. MY BROTHER ALF SERVED IN MANY LOCATIONS THROUGHOUT VIETNAM AS A MOBILE RADIO OPERATOR. THEY, ALONG WITH COUNTLESS OTHER AMERICAN SERVICE MEMBERS, WERE EXPOSED TO AGENT ORANGE, A DEFOLIANT USED TO QUICKLY ELIMINATE TRIPLE CANOPY JUNGLE MAKING IT HARDER FOR THE VIET CONG TO HIDE. IT WAS IN THE WATER THEY DRANK AND IN THE SHOWERS THEY TOOK. AGENT ORANGE SEEPED INTO THE SOLDIERS FROM THE INSIDE AND OUTSIDE. BOTH ALF AND DAVID GOT CANCER AND DIED.

THE NAME ORANGE CRUSH COMES FROM THE PROCESS OF EXTRACTING OILS FROM ORANGES. ONE OF THE INVENTORS OF ORANGE CRUSH WAS A CHEMIST. MONSANTO AND DOW WERE TWO OF THE COMPANIES WHO PRODUCED AGENT ORANGE FOR USE IN VIETNAM. THE BAND REM CAME OUT WITH A SONG CALLED "ORANGE CRUSH" ON THEIR GREEN ALBUM IN 1988. I ALWAYS LIKED THE SONG, BUT IT WAS NOT UNTIL 2022 THAT I DISCOVERED WHAT THE SONG WAS ABOUT. THE LEAD SINGER MICHAEL STIPE GREW UP IN A MILITARY FAMILY. HIS DAD, WHO DIED IN 2015, SERVED AS A HELICOPTER PILOT IN VIETNAM. THE SONG REFERS TO AGENT ORANGE CRUSHING THE HOPES AND DREAMS OF MILLIONS OF PEOPLE.

US AIR FORCE C-123 PLANES, AS PART OF OPERATION RANCH HAND, SPRAYED 20 MILLION GALLONS OF AGENT ORANGE ON SOUTH VIETNAM. AS A PARODY OF THE SMOKEY THE BEAR SLOGAN, THE PILOTS HAD THEIR OWN SLOGAN: "ONLY YOU CAN PREVENT A FOREST."

ORANGE CRUSH BY REM

(FOLLOW ME, DON'T FOLLOW ME)
I'VE GOT MY SPINE, I'VE GOT MY ORANGE CRUSH
(COLLAR ME, DON'T COLLAR ME)
I'VE GOT MY SPINE, I'VE GOT MY ORANGE CRUSH
(WE ARE AGENTS OF THE FREE)
I'VE HAD MY FUN AND NOW IT'S TIME TO SERVE YOUR CONSCIENCE OVERSEAS
(OVER ME, NOT OVER ME)
COMING IN FAST, OVER ME (OH, OH)

Hyperosmia

STORY BY BRUCE OLAV SOLHEIM PH.D. * ART BY TETIANA HORINA

New Oriental Lime

Use too much and you can find yourself in a tight squeeze.

I'VE NEVER BEEN ABLE TO WEAR AFTERSHAVE BECAUSE MY NOSE IS MUCH TOO SENSITIVE. I GUESS I'M MISSING OUT.

WHEN I WAS WORKING IN BOTH MILITARY AND CIVILIAN PRISONS, MY HYPEROSMIA WAS A PROBLEM. A THOUSAND CRIMINALS KEPT IN CAGES GENERATES A STENCH THAT YOU CAN NEVER FORGET.

HEY, GUARD, CAN I GET A FLUSH ON TWELVE?

THE BIGGEST ADVANTAGE OF HAVING HYPEROSMIA IS THAT IT ULTIMATELY INCREASES ONE'S CHANCE OF SURVIVAL. A PERSON WITH AN ENHANCED OLFACTORY SYSTEM CAN LITERALLY SMELL DANGER. FOR EXAMPLE, DURING THE VIETNAM WAR, LONG RANGE RECONNAISSANCE PATROLS (LRPS) COULD DETECT THE ENEMY THROUGH THEIR LINGERING AFTERSHAVE OR CIGARETTE SMOKE (MENTHOL BEING THE EASIEST TO DETECT). THIS SKILL IS OBVIOUSLY IMPORTANT IN WAR. OFTEN, WHEN ORDINARY PEOPLE SENSE THAT SOMETHING DOESN'T FEEL QUITE RIGHT, THEY ARE ALERTED THROUGH ALL THEIR SENSES, INCLUDING SMELL.

DUGNAD

Story by Bruce Olav Solheim, Ph.D.   Art by Luiz Rosa

"PARDON ME, WE JUST WANT TO KNOW HOW WE CAN HELP YOU GUYS AROUND HERE."

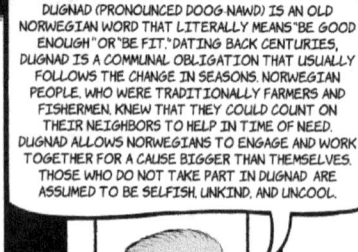

DUGNAD (PRONOUNCED DOOG-NAWD) IS AN OLD NORWEGIAN WORD THAT LITERALLY MEANS "BE GOOD ENOUGH" OR "BE FIT." DATING BACK CENTURIES, DUGNAD IS A COMMUNAL OBLIGATION THAT USUALLY FOLLOWS THE CHANGE IN SEASONS. NORWEGIAN PEOPLE, WHO WERE TRADITIONALLY FARMERS AND FISHERMEN, KNEW THAT THEY COULD COUNT ON THEIR NEIGHBORS TO HELP IN TIME OF NEED. DUGNAD ALLOWS NORWEGIANS TO ENGAGE AND WORK TOGETHER FOR A CAUSE BIGGER THAN THEMSELVES. THOSE WHO DO NOT TAKE PART IN DUGNAD ARE ASSUMED TO BE SELFISH, UNKIND, AND UNCOOL.

"BE GOOD ENOUGH TO EARN YOUR PLACE IN SOCIETY."

GARUDA

STORY BY BRUCE OLAV SOLHEIM, PH.D. **ART BY HUSNI ASSAEROZI**

I HAD YET ANOTHER LUCID DREAM VISION. I WAS MEETING WITH MY FRIEND AND WORLD-RENOWNED PARAPSYCHOLOGIST JEFFREY MISHLOVE, WHO IS THE CREATOR OF NEW THINKING ALLOWED.

HEY BRUCE. THANK YOU FOR BEING HERE. I HAVE A SURPRISE FOR YOU. THESE ARE TWO VERY SPECIAL STATUES THAT I WANT YOU TO CONCENTRATE ON... WHEN YOU ARE READY, TOUCH BOTH OF THEM SIMULTANEOUSLY.

GARUDA

STORY BY BRUCE OLAV SOLHEIM, PH.D.　　　**ART BY HUSNI ASSAEROZI**

I HAD YET ANOTHER LUCID DREAM VISION. I WAS MEETING WITH MY FRIEND AND WORLD-RENOWNED PARAPSYCHOLOGIST JEFFREY MISHLOVE, WHO IS THE CREATOR OF NEW THINKING ALLOWED.

HEY BRUCE. THANK YOU FOR BEING HERE. I HAVE A SURPRISE FOR YOU. THESE ARE TWO VERY SPECIAL STATUES THAT I WANT YOU TO CONCENTRATE ON... WHEN YOU ARE READY, TOUCH BOTH OF THEM SIMULTANEOUSLY.

MISTER MOTORCYCLE MAN

STORY BY BRUCE OLAV SOLHEIM, PH.D * ART BY ERICK REYES

IT HAD BEEN 37 YEARS SINCE I LAST RODE, BUT I WAS UNDETERRED. I TRIED A TRIUMPH SPEEDMASTER, BUT SOON SETTLED ON A HARLEY—A HERITAGE CLASSIC. IT WAS A SUBSTANTIAL INVESTMENT OF MONEY THAT I SOON CAME TO REGRET. BUT I DID NOT STOP THERE. NO, I DECIDED TO JOIN A MOTORCYCLE CLUB OR MC. I THOUGHT IT WOULD BE A CLEVER IDEA TO FIND A VETERAN MC, SO I CALLED AND SPOKE TO A GUY NAMED WHIPLASH. HE MADE A POINT OF ASKING ME IF I HAD EVER BEEN IN LAW ENFORCEMENT. I TOLD HIM THAT I HAD WORKED AS A GUARD IN A MAXIMUM SECURITY PRISON IN MINNESOTA FROM 1982-83.

WHILE I WAS LOOKING FOR AN MC THAT WOULD ACCEPT ME, I RODE AROUND IN MY FULL RIDING GEAR, AT LEAST LOOKING THE PART. ONE DAY, I RODE TO THE GROCERY STORE TO GET MY WIFE GINGER SOME MILK. THE BOY SCOUTS WERE OUT IN FRONT OF THE STORE SELLING SOMETHING. THEY APPROACHED ME, AND I TOLD THEM I DIDN'T WANT TO BUY ANYTHING. THE BRATTY KID REALLY PUT ME IN MY PLACE.

AFTER WATCHING SONS OF ANARCHY, I REALIZED THERE WAS NO WAY I COULD BE A MEMBER OF SUCH AN OUTLAW MC. INSTEAD, I FOUND AN MC THAT HAD SOME VETERANS AND WAS DEDICATED TO HELPING VETERANS. A FORMER VETERAN STUDENT OF MINE WAS IN THE CLUB AND VOUCHED FOR ME.

THE PROCESS FOR JOINING AN MC:

1. HANG-AROUND PHASE
2. PROSPECT PHASE
3. FULL CLUB MEMBER

AS A PROSPECT FOR AN MC, I WAS ASKED TO DO ALL THE DIRTY WORK AND GOT LITTLE RESPECT. THERE WERE LOTS OF RULES AS WELL. I HAD TO GET DRINKS FOR THE PATCHED MEMBERS, CLEAN THEIR BIKES, AND RUN ERRANDS, DAY, AND NIGHT. I WAS MADE TO ATTEND THE CONFEDERATION OF CLUBS (COC) MEETINGS. THE COC MEETINGS INCLUDED BOTH OUTLAW, SO-CALLED "ONE-PERCENTER" CLUBS, AND REGULAR MC'S. I BEGAN TO SLOWLY REALIZE THAT OUR MC MIGHT BE AN AFFILIATE BECAUSE OUTLAW MC'S WOULD BE AT OUR EVENTS AND ONE OF OUR PATCHED MEMBERS HAD A BROTHER IN A "ONE-PERCENTER" MC.

ISN'T YOUR BROTHER IN AN OUTLAW MC?

THERE'S NO SUCH THING AS OUTLAW CLUBS. WE'RE ALL JUST MOTORCYCLE ENTHUSIASTS, GET IT?

WHAT AM I DOING?

HE WAS CRAZY AND A LIAR. THE NEXT DAY, A TRUCK SWERVED IN FRONT OF ME TRYING TO RUN ME OFF THE ROAD. PERHAPS A RIVAL CLUB? MY OLD SCHOOL PROSPECT PATCH MADE ME A TARGET OF OUTLAW CLUBS WHO MIGHT THINK I WAS A RIVAL. ALSO, MY MC HAD AN ENCRYPTED MESSAGE SYSTEM FOR WHICH I WASN'T CLEARED. SKETCHY SHIT WAS GOING ON. THEN, GINGER TOLD ME: "FOR A BUNCH OF GUYS WHO CLAIM TO LOVE THEIR FREEDOM AND RIDING MOTORCYCLES, THEY SURE HAVE A LOT OF RULES!" SHE WAS RIGHT! WHAT I THOUGHT BEING IN AN MC WOULD BE LIKE, WAS NOT WHAT IT WAS. THE FANTASY WAS OVER.

FET DOG

STORY BY BRUCE OLAV SOLHEIM, PH.D. / ART BY ZIMESS

I LOST MY BROTHER IN 2023, JUST BEFORE CHRISTMAS. WITH MY PARENTS AND MY SISTER GONE, I'M NOW THE LAST ONE—ALONE. I SPENT SEVERAL WEEKS IN THE SEATTLE AREA VISITING MY BROTHER WHILE HE WAS IN THE HOSPITAL. I HAD TIME TO THINK AND TO EXPLORE, AND WHAT I SAW DEEPLY DISAPPOINTED ME. EVERYWHERE I WENT, I SAW URBAN AND SUBURBAN DECAY—HOMELESSNESS, OVER-CROWDING, POVERTY, AND DESPAIR. MUCH HAD CHANGED SINCE I MOVED TO SOUTHERN CALIFORNIA IN 1998.

MY BROTHER AND I TALKED ABOUT GROWING UP IN SEATTLE. OUR DAD WAS A HARD-WORKING FISHERMAN AND CARPENTER, AND OUR MOM WAS A HOME MAKER AND ARTIST. IN MANY WAYS IT WAS AN IDYLLIC LIFE. BUT THE VIETNAM WAR CHANGED THAT FOR MY BROTHER WHEN HE VOLUNTEERED TO JOIN THE US AIR FORCE IN 1967.

ANOTHER DEADLY CHEMICAL KNOWN AS FENTANYL IS NOW KILLING PEOPLE WHERE WE GREW UP. NOT FAR FROM THE HOSPITAL WHERE MY BROTHER LAY, I SAW AN UNCONSCIOUS, HOMELESS DRUG ADDICT IN FRONT OF AN ABANDONED 7-11 STORE.

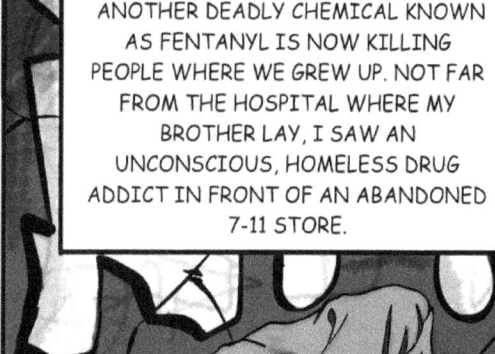

HOW COULD HE HAVE KNOWN THAT 56 YEARS LATER, A DEFOLIANT USED IN THE WAR CALLED AGENT ORANGE WOULD KILL HIM?

$C_4H_4O_2$

$C_{22}H_{28}O$

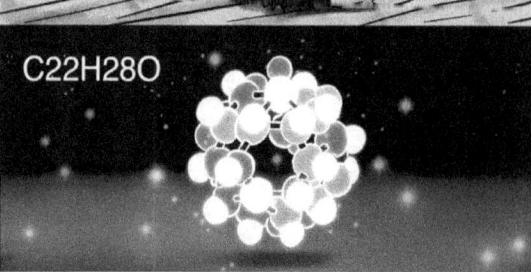

DUST OFF

STORY BY BRUCE OLAV SOLHEIM, PH.D. * ART BY TETIANA HORINA

ON THE EPIPHANY, JANUARY 6, 2025, I ARRIVED ON CAMPUS EARLY FOR THE FIRST DAY OF THE WINTER SEMESTER. THE CAMPUS WAS QUIET AND NEARLY EMPTY, WITH ONLY A FEW CARS IN THE PARKING LOT AND A HANDFUL OF PEOPLE WALKING AROUND THE SPACIOUS GROUNDS.

THIS IS ME BACK IN 2000 WHEN I FOUNDED THE VETERANS PROGRAM AT CITRUS COLLEGE.

I WAS NERVOUS, BUT THAT WAS NORMAL FOR THE FIRST DAY. I'M A NATURAL INTROVERT WHO OFTEN SUFFERS FROM STAGE FRIGHT. I PRAYED THAT I WOULD BE AN EFFECTIVE TEACHER AND ROLE MODEL FOR MY STUDENTS, GUIDING THEM ON THEIR LIFE JOURNEY. TEACHING IS A SERIOUS AND SACRED RESPONSIBILITY. I HAVE WORKED AT CITRUS COLLEGE SINCE 1998.

EVEN THOUGH ALL WAS QUIET, I APPROACHED THE STAIRCASE WITH INCREASING ANXIETY. THEN, AT THE BOTTOM OF THE LANDING FROM THE SECOND FLOOR, I SAW A YOUNG STUDENT SPRAWLED OUT AT THE BOTTOM. I THOUGHT HE WAS DEAD UNTIL I SAW SIGNS OF BREATHING, BUT HE WAS INJURED AND BLEEDING.

"HEY, BUDDY, ARE YOU OKAY?" I SAID. HE BEGAN TO STIR AND SAT UP. BEFORE I COULD SAY ANYTHING ELSE, HE GRABBED THE TWO CANS OF DUST OFF (USED TO CLEAN COMPUTERS) AND SPRAYED THE CHEMICALS DIRECTLY INTO HIS NOSTRILS.

"HEY! STOP THAT! IT'S NOT GOOD FOR YOU!" I YELLED IN MY DAD VOICE. HE GOT UP AND STAGGERED AWAY. I TRIED TO CALL SECURITY, BUT HE STARTED RUNNING, SO I DECIDED TO FOLLOW HIM INSTEAD. HE FINALLY CAME TO REST IN BETWEEN TWO BUILDINGS. SITTING IN THE DIRT, HE WAS HUFFING FROM THE TWO CANS AGAIN. I GOT AHOLD OF SECURITY AND THEY CALLED AN AMBULANCE. HE WAS SO YOUNG.

I THOUGHT ABOUT MY DREAM OF BEING A "DUST OFF" PILOT IN THE ARMY (MEDICAL EVACUATION) AND HOW I ENDED UP IN AN AIR CAVALRY UNIT INSTEAD. DISILLUSIONMENT LED ME INTO A DOWNWARD SPIRAL. I DID SOME RESEARCH AND FOUND OUT THE CHEMICAL IN DUST OFF IS HIGHLY ADDICTIVE AND THAT ABUSE OF INHALANTS (HUFFING) IS A BIG TREND WITH YOUNG PEOPLE. WHAT SAD THING HAD HAPPENED TO THIS YOUNG MAN THAT LED HIM TO THIS ADDICTION? I HOPE THAT I HELPED.

MY FINAL CHAPTER

Story by Bruce Olav Solheim, Ph.D. — Art by Julia Kazanowska

NOW, AT THE AGE OF 66, I'M TAKING INVENTORY AND DECIDING WHAT IS WORTH MY TIME IN WHATEVER TIME I HAVE LEFT. I PLAN ON LIVING TO BE 124, BUT YOU NEVER KNOW. I'VE BEGUN EXPLORING PARTS OF MY LIFE THAT I'VE HERETOFORE LEFT UNEXPLORED. THIS INVENTORY HAS INCLUDED MANY PARANORMAL EXPERIENCES AND ALIEN CONTACT THAT I'VE COVERED IN MY TIMELESS TRILOGY, ANZAR THE PROGENITOR, WE ARE THE ALIENS, AND THROUGH FICTIONAL CHARACTERS IN MY SNARC AND DR. JEKYLL ALIEN HUNTER COMIC BOOKS.

NATIVE AMERICANS ARE A BIG PART OF MY LIFE STORY AND HAVE ALWAYS BEEN A SOURCE OF INSPIRATION AND WISDOM FOR ME.

PREPARING TO DIE, OLD LODGE SKINS, PLAYED BY CHIEF DAN GEORGE IN THE 1971 FILM LITTLE BIG MAN, SAID: "COME OUT AND FIGHT, IT IS A GOOD DAY TO DIE. THANK YOU FOR MAKING ME A HUMAN BEING. THANK YOU FOR HELPING ME BECOME A WARRIOR. THANK YOU FOR MY VICTORIES AND FOR MY DEFEATS." MESSAGE RECEIVED.

I'VE MET MANY NATIVE AMERICANS WHO HAVE TAUGHT ME AND GUIDED ME. THE FIRST WAS THE INDIAN AT THE PUYALLUP FAIR IN 1966 WHO TAUGHT ME HOW TO WALK WITH RESPECT UPON THE EARTH.

IN 1978, I MET AN ALEUT NAMED HANK, WHO BEFRIENDED ME IN SOUTH NAKNEK, ALASKA.

WILLY, AN INUPIAT VIETNAM VETERAN SAVED ME FROM A POLAR BEAR IN POINT BARROW, ALASKA, IN 1993.

I CAN'T FORGET PHIL RED EAGLE, THE VIETNAM VETERAN AND AUTHOR WHO TOLD ME I WAS A MYSTIC SEER IN 1996.

LEON, A SPIRIT WORLD MEDICINE MAN, CAME TO ME IN A VISION WHILE I WAS CAMPING AT MOUNT ADAMS IN WASHINGTON STATE IN 1993. HE SANG TO ME AND SHOWED ME TREETOP WARRIORS.

NATIVE AMERICANS AND OTHER INDIGENOUS PEOPLE CALL ALIENS STAR PEOPLE AND RECOGNIZE THAT WE LIVE IN A WORLD WHERE THE PARANORMAL IS NORMAL AND THE SUPERNATURAL IS NATURAL. FOR MODERN SOCIETY, IT'S SCIENCE FICTION, FOR NATIVE AMERICANS, IT HAS ALWAYS BEEN THEIR REALITY. I'M MORE SPIRITUAL NOW THAN EVER. I THINK THAT THESE EXPERIENCES I'VE HAD WITH NATIVE AMERICAN TEACHERS WERE PREPARING ME FOR WHAT LIES AHEAD. I'M NOT TOTALLY SURE WHAT IT IS, BUT I SUSPECT IT WILL BE BEAUTIFUL!

CONCLUSION

The End of Our Elaborate Plans

I've always been drawn to the song "The End" by The Doors. Its haunting melody and lyrics are used to great effect in Francis Ford Coppola's brilliant film *Apocalypse Now*, which is based on Joseph Conrad's novel *Heart of Darkness*. Jim Morrison's poignant words resonate deeply:

This is the end
Beautiful friend
This is the end
My only friend, the end
Of our elaborate plans, the end
Of everything that stands, the end
No safety or surprise, the end
I'll never look into your eyes again

Coincidentally, we've come to the end of *Gig Line*. I hope you've enjoyed it, dear reader. If you want to get in touch with any of the artists, just email me (contact information is in my bio). They're all delightfully brilliant!

As I mentioned in the introduction, I'm fascinated by how other people see me and how artists draw me. Am I a chameleon? More importantly, the visual nuances each artist brings out add significantly to the meaning of each story and chronologically propel us through the narrative. I believe that each person we meet in life has something to teach us. These teachers, however, aren't always pleasant or friendly, and the lessons are often fraught with danger, heartache, and pain.

Have you ever wondered how deeply the military and war can shape a person's life? From my mom and dad's harrowing stories of living under Nazi occupation in Norway to my brother's grueling tours of duty in Vietnam and, finally, my own US Army Cold War service from 1978 to 1986, human conflict has left a permanent imprint on me. And it's not over because my eldest son Bjørn is still in the US Air Force after twenty-five years of service. The military and war have indelibly marked me and my development as a man.

Some of my other stories delve into my experiences working in both military and civilian prisons. The parallels are undeniable. Such environments shaped my worldview, and I've learned to navigate life's challenges through a lens tinted by tragedy and conflict. The most profound lesson I've learned is that we're all both warriors and peacemakers, as Swiss psychoanalyst Carl Jung described when he spoke of the duality of man. The key is to know when and where the warrior should emerge.

I've taught college-level history since 1990. How lucky am I to get to tell stories for a living? I've taught and written history with a personal approach. As I often say, "History begins and ends with the individual." For example, when America goes to war, America doesn't go to war. Individual Americans go to war. Collectively, our personal stories form the fabric of our national history, and then each national history forms the fabric of global history.

As I've learned my life lessons, I've grown as a teacher. Much of this growth has come through interactions with my students. As the German expressionist artist Paul Klee once said, "It is the teacher and not the student who should pay tuition."

There is something about me that none of my students, friends, family, or even my wife knows. Every day, I cry because I miss my mom and dad, and my brother and sister. I'm alone, in a sense, and there is no one in my family older than me with whom I can consult. History is about loss. If you live long enough, you'll lose many loved ones. I'm sure that war and military service have shortened the lives of my immediate family members, either directly or indirectly. It'll likely shorten mine.

Because I teach American history, I teach about war. In doing so, I'm teaching what I want to know. For instance, how did we get into the Vietnam War, and what have we learned from that experience? I never fought in Vietnam, but my life journey has been touched by those who did and by the lingering effects of that war. Both my brother Alf and my best friend and writing mentor David Willson died in the past few years due to exposure to Agent Orange while serving in South Vietnam in the 1960s. As historian Ernest Lefever said, "Vietnam won't go away . . . Its ghosts still haunt the American psyche like fragments of a twisted nightmare."

We must all share our stories and connections so that students can begin to see their roots and connection to the war and its impact. Personal histories and our journeys bring events to life for our students. We must remember the power of the story. Our ancestors taught through oral tradition for many thousands of years before writing was invented. It's in our blood. It's our penitence to retell the story of the Vietnam War. We have it in us to heal from wars if we can just wake up from our historical amnesia and remember where it all begins and ends.

In a 1963 publication put out by The American Friends of Vietnam, a private advocacy group that worked to influence US war policy, they said more than they knew when they wrote that "Americans do not realize how much of that faraway place is in all of us." Native Americans believe that through engaging in war, you experience soul loss. That is why returned warriors would go through sweat lodge ceremonies to heal and be reborn. In modern society, we don't understand this wisdom, and our veterans suffer as a result.

Now, we're at the end, and I'd like to return to my initial question in the introduction: What is *Gig Line*? I believe *Gig Line* presents my growth as a man and a human being, seeking alignment and balance in a chaotic world. I've discovered that when you're on the right track, with your goals and values in balance and alignment, the universe seemingly works with you instead of against you. My mentor, Harvey Pekar (also a military veteran), sought balance and alignment as he struggled in life. Even his success toward the end of his life didn't bring him the healing he wanted. I sympathize with his lifelong battle with depression. Ironically, it was an accidental overdose of his anti-depressants that killed him.

Like many military veterans, I suffer from post-traumatic stress disorder (PTSD) and depression, enough to where I contemplated taking my own life. Luckily, the Veterans Administration (VA) provided top-notch counseling and medical care, and I'm doing fine nowadays. Synchronicities abound now that I'm on the right path, in alignment, and maintaining a delicate balance as I slip into my golden years.

In the introduction, I wrote about the purpose of this book, which is to seek peace and cooperation among people through comics. The artists in this book are from different countries, ideologies, religions, genders, and races—which are often things that divide us. Some of them live in the middle of a war zone, yet they continue their creative work despite the danger and hardship. I believe this demonstrates the indomitable creative human spirit and shared humanity that comic books can represent. As President John F. Kennedy said on June 10, 1963, shortly before his assassination:

> *So, let us not be blind to our differences, but let us also direct attention to our common interests and the means by which those differences can be resolved. And if we cannot end now our differences, at least we can help make the world safe for diversity. For, in the final analysis, our most basic common link is that we all inhabit this small planet. We all breathe the same air. We all cherish our children's future. And we are all mortal.*

Our shared humanity, despite our differences, is the basis of our kinship. Yet, to our own detriment, we tend to ever increasingly focus on those things that divide us. Modern life seems quite Kafkaesque. As my dear departed friend David Willson always said, "No good deed goes unpunished." Modern technology has isolated us even as it has opened the entire world to us. You can see people walking around with their heads down, focusing intently on their phones, while other human beings pass by almost unnoticed. It's no wonder that magic, ghost-hunting shows, and UFOs are more popular now than ever—people are looking for a connection to something bigger than themselves.

From the spirit world, David has reached out to me with some sage advice: "Talk to the living. You'll have plenty of time to talk to us later." His dark humor shines through, giving me pause to consider what is most important: engaging with the human beings around me.

My friend Viet Thanh Nguyen, a Pulitzer Prize-winning Vietnamese refugee, once wrote, "All wars are fought twice, the first time on the battlefield, the second time in memory." It's my job as a historian to teach about war. I don't have a time machine that can transport my students to the jungles of Vietnam, the trenches of France, or the beach at Iwo Jima, but I do have personal narratives, oral histories, films, and an understanding of the paradox of war. It's a formidable responsibility to be fair and inclusive, but not so much so that you avoid controversy or conjecture. We're not timid creatures, and we all seek the truth. History writing is a messy business, and these histories can evolve over time. What I believed to be true when I was twenty-five years old isn't exactly what I believe to be true today. Everything that has happened has been preparation for the next thing. "Ordinary life is pretty complex stuff," as Harvey Pekar once wrote. And I would add—we must be kind to others and to ourselves because we're doing our best until our elaborate plans in life come to an end. No one can judge us without truly knowing what we've faced in life, just as we can't judge others without having walked a mile in their shoes, as my mom often told me. Harvey Pekar wrote, "I think that the so-called average person often exhibits a great deal of heroism in getting through an ordinary day." I agree with Harvey as I've come to the same conclusion: We're all heroes in our own life stories, my dear reader, my beautiful friend.

BRUCE OLAV SOLHEIM, PH.D.

Bruce Olav Solheim was born in Seattle, Washington, to Norwegian immigrant parents. A disabled veteran, he served for six years in the US Army as a jail guard in West Germany, and later as a warrant officer helicopter pilot at the 82nd Airborne Division. As a civilian, Solheim worked as a defense contractor at Boeing for five years, then went on to earn his Ph.D. in history from Bowling Green State University in 1993, with his main field being US foreign policy. Bruce was the first person in his family to go to college and is currently a distinguished professor of history at Citrus College in Glendora, California, where he has taught for 27 years. As a Fulbright Professor and Scholar, Dr. Solheim taught at the University of Tromsø in northern Norway in 2003.

In 2001, Dr. Solheim founded the veterans program at Citrus College and, in 2007, co-founded (along with Ginger De Villa-Rose and former East Los Angeles Vet Center Director Manuel Martinez) the first in the nation college transition course for recently returned veterans called Boots to Books.

A prolific writer, Solheim has published thirteen books and written ten plays, six of which have been produced. In addition to his academic books/journal/novel *(The Nordic Nexus: A Lesson in Peaceful Security*, *On Top of the World: Women's Political Leadership in Scandinavia and Beyond*, *Viet Nam Generation Journal*, *Women in Power: World Leaders since 1960*, *The Vietnam War Era: A Personal Journey*, *Ali's Bees*, *Making History: A Personal Approach to Modern American History*, and *I'm An American: A Personal Approach to Early American History)*, he has published several books about the paranormal. In fact, Dr. Solheim teaches a Paranormal Personal History course at Citrus College.

Alongside his list of published works, Solheim has also published two comic book series. *Snarc* (issues 1 and 2) features an alien hybrid character of the same name, and *Dr. Jekyll Alien Hunter* (issues 1 and 2) with a female lead character. His latest comic book is called *Gig Line: A Comic Book Autobiography*. Bruce is married to Ginger (a small business owner and helicopter certified flight instructor) and has four accomplished children (a US Air Force master sergeant, an engineer, a registered nurse (RN), and an electrician), and two grandsons.

Email: bsolheim@citruscollege.edu or bootstobooks@gmail.com
Website: www.bruceolavsolheim.com

JULIA KAZANOWSKA

Julia is a small artist from Poland. Drawing has been her passion since early childhood. Art is a huge part of her life, and she does it almost every time she can. She works full-time as a 2D game artist and part-time as a comic illustrator. She's obsessed with comics (especially manga) and games. Creating graphics for the two media she loves the most is one of the biggest joys of her life.

GEORGE VERONGOS

George Verongos was born and raised in the Midwest, where he developed a lifelong love of books and music. A high school dropout, George went on to graduate from the Evergreen State College in 1995, with concentrations in audio engineering, ethnomusicology, and modern American literature. After a few years of playing in bands, he undertook postbaccalaureate studies in secondary English education at Indiana University South Bend while working at his family's restaurant. After earning his teaching license, Verongos taught English and writing from New Jersey to Oregon and a few points in between. In 2010, George founded LiteraryServices.net, which is dedicated to providing independent authors access to professional publishing services. Since then, George has edited many books, including works by bestselling and award-winning authors such as Terry Lovelace and Dr. Bruce Solheim. In addition, he has written and published a collection of short stories based on his childhood called *My Dad is Dead and Other Funny Stories*. He also co-wrote a screenplay with Lovelace based on his bestselling book, *Incident at Devil's Den*. Verongos currently lives in the magical Northwest with his partner Zoë and their feline overlord, Baba Ghanoush.

Email: LitServEditor@gmail.com

Website: www.LiteraryServices.net

www.ingramcontent.com/pod-product-compliance
Lightning Source LLC
LaVergne TN
LVHW081453060526
838201LV00050BA/1783